CAMBODIA: A MATTER OF SURVIVAL

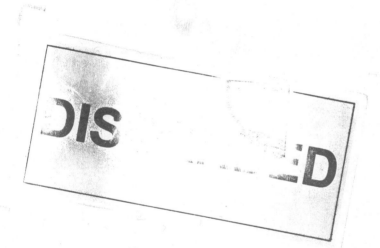

CAMBODIA: A MATTER OF SURVIVAL

COUNTRIES IN CRISIS

Edited by

MARTIN WRIGHT

**Contributors: Charles McGregor,
John Pedler, Darren Sagar
Frances D'Souza, Martin Wright**

Longman

CAMBODIA: A MATTER OF SURVIVAL

Published by Longman Group UK Limited,
Westgate House, The High, Harlow, Essex CM20 1YR, UK.
Telephone (0279) 442601
Telex 81491 Padlog
Facsimile (0279) 444501

Published in the United States and Canada by St James Press,
233 East Ontario St, Chicago 60611, Illinois, U.S.A.

ISBN 0-582-05157-6 (Longman, hard cover)
      0-582-05159-2 (Longman, paper cover)

      1-55862-047-8   (St James)

First published in 1989

British Library Cataloguing in Publication Data
Cambodia: a matter of survival (Countries in crisis).
   1. Kampuchea. Political events, history
   I. McGregor, Charles II. Wright, Martin, 1958– III.
   Series
   959.6

   ISBN 0–582–05157–6
   ISBN 0–582–05159–2 pbk

Phototypeset by Quorn Selective Repro Ltd, Loughborough, Leics.
Printed and bound in Great Britain by
Biddles Ltd, Guildford and King's Lynn

CONTENTS

ABOUT THE AUTHORS

Charles McGregor has worked as research associate at the International Institute of Strategic Studies and as Writer for the BBC Far Eastern Service. He is author of the 1988 Adelphi Paper, *The Sino-Vietnamese Relationship and the Soviet Union*.

John Pedler served as a British diplomat in Indochina, including a period in Phnom Penh during the Sihanouk years, before becoming a journalist, reporting on Vietnam and Cambodia for numerous publications including *The Times*.

Darren Sagar writes on South East Asian affairs for *Keesing's Record of World Events*. He is author of *Major Political Events in Indo-China, 1945–89*, to be published by *Facts On File* in 1990.

Frances D'Souza was founder of the Relief and Development Institute, Lecturer at the London School of Economics and Senior Academic Visitor at Oxford University. She is currently Director of Article 19, the international centre on censorship.

Martin Wright is Editor of the *Countries in Crisis* series. Formerly on the staff of *Keesing's Record of World Events*, he now works as a freelance journalist and publishing consultant.

PREFACE

For nearly 20 years, the ancient Khmer land of *Kambuja*—Kampuchea, Cambodia, call it what you will—has been a media catchphrase for helplessness and horror. After being dragged into war and the spotlight of world attention by America's adventures in Vietnam, systematically slaughtered in the killing fields of the *Khmer Rouge*, and then kicked around in a game of power politics between China, Moscow and the West, Cambodians are, once again, finding themselves facing another war fuelled and sustained from abroad.

This book presents a clear-cut, highly readable survey of the perils and prospects facing Cambodia today, in the wake of the failed Paris peace initiatives. In Part I, a detailed history traces Cambodia's fortunes from its earliest days through to the twists and turns of the latest peace talks.

Part II features assessments by leading commentators of the state of Cambodia today, and of the prospects for eventual peace and reconciliation. It focuses on the endeavours of Cambodians themselves, and on the involvement—sometimes valuable, often disastrous—of the world at large. In so doing, it provides some pointers as to how—and why—this little-known country became sucked into the maelstrom of international politics.

Individual briefings cover the prospects for a diplomatic settlement, the politics of aid, and the military balance of the rival armed forces—including the most comprehensive assessment ever published of the real strength and threat posed by the newly "respectable" *Khmers Rouges*.

A reference section groups together key facts and figures, including a detailed breakdown of the numerous political factions and guerrilla groups.

Acknowledgements. The Editor would like to extend his thanks to John Pedler for his valuable advice during the initial stages of the project.

The front cover photograph, by David Modell, was provided by the Select Photo Agency. Permission for the use of this photo and others appearing in the text by Jill Arace, Pete Brabban, David Munro and Mike Youde (all for Oxfam) is gratefully acknowledged. Copyright remains with the agencies/photographers. Thanks are also due to CARPRESS International Press Agency for providing the map on p. viii.

CAMBODIA: INFRASTRUCTURE

Cambodia is situated in South-East Asia; in the south-western part of the Indo-Chinese peninsular. Covering an area of over 180,000 sq km, it is bordered on the west and north-west by Thailand, on the north-east by Laos and on the east and south-east by Vietnam. Along the south and south-west, the provinces of Koh Kong and Kampot face the Gulf of Thailand.

Cambodia's main topographical features are the Mekong River and the *Tonle Sap* ("the Great Lake"), a large inland sea surrounded by a broad plain. The Mekong enters Cambodia from Laos and flows broadly southwards to the border with Vietnam. During the rainy season (June to October) the overflow from the Mekong runs back up the connecting river to the *Tonle Sap*, reversing its course, and causing the lake to expand to several times its dry season size. As the water level of the Mekong falls, the process is reversed. As a result of this annual phenomenon, the *Tonle Sap* is one of the world's richest sources of fresh-water fish. To the south-west stand low mountain chains, including the Cardomom and Elephant mountains, while the northern rim of the country is bounded by the Phanom Dang Raek uplands, with a prominent sandstone escarpment.

Cambodia's considerable agricultural potential has remained largely untapped, large parts of the country having been a battle zone for the best part of 40 years. Nevertheless, the country is rich in timber and fish and, if the Mekong were properly harnessed, large, submerged areas of the central plain could be used for the growing of rice and other crops. In addition, the damming of the Mekong could provide the country with sufficient electricity for its own needs and, as in the case of neighbouring Laos, a surplus for export.

THE PEOPLE

Over 90 per cent of Cambodia's population are ethnic Khmer. The only significant ethnic minority are the Moslem Cham, although other Khmerized ethnic groups including the *Kuy* and *Pear* exist in small numbers.

Before the 1970s there were considerable Chinese and Vietnamese communities living in Cambodia. Virtually all the Vietnamese were killed or expelled between 1970 and 1979. A number of new Vietnamese settlers have returned following the installation of the pro-Vietnam People's Republic of Kampuchea (PRK) regime in 1979. The exact size of the new Vietnamese community is disputed, and some commentators have accused Hanoi of carrying out a policy of "Vietnamization" in Cambodia. The number of urban Chinese fell dramatically under the *Khmer Rouge's* regime (1975–78), and most of those who survived the rigours of the Pol Pot era emigrated during the first months of pro-Vietnam PRK rule.

Looking to the future in Prey Veng province *(Mike Youde/Oxfam)*

A grim memorial to the victims of the Khmers Rouges *(David Munro/Oxfam)*

REPORTAGE

ON THE ROAD

John Pedler

Travelling by road in Cambodia is often uncomfortable, but it can at times be hilarious. Cambodians have commonly a whimsical, rather British, sense of humour and tend to enjoy inventing an improbably funny scene which two or three of them vie with each other to embroider with ever more unlikely—and sometimes macabre—absurdities. Horror lies just beneath the surface—the 10 year old memories of Pol Pot are still too fresh. As we drove along the road from Battambang towards the beleaguered gem mines at Pailin my "minder" told me of "the forest people"—the unquiet spirits of the unburied dead which nowadays abound in Cambodia. This seriously disquiets a great many Cambodians who spend much time in both Buddhist and animistic rites to placate them.

Hearing mention of this sombre fact, our chauffeur drolly invented a group of "forest people" who, like most up-and-coming Cambodians, wanted to brush up on their French and English. My minder, not to be outdone in whimsy, hastened to explain that it was because the "forest people" were so anxious to listen in on our chit-chat that the car—then negotiating potholes a foot deep—was obliged to go so slowly. Not so, said the chauffeur—he could drive no faster because there were some "car spirits" among the "forest people"—Pol Pot hated cars and smashed them wilfully leaving them to rust unburied where they lay. It was the car spirits who were detaining us, the chauffeur explained, as they were so happy to find another car to chat to after all the dreary lorries that used the road to take gem prospectors to and from Pailin. And so the whimsy grew, our laughter at each absurdity passing the time and easing the anxieties of an uncertain road.

Only the two vital main roads, linking Phnom Penh to Saigon and to the one true seaport of Kompong Som are completely asphalted—apart from a bridge or two. All other roads have long sections of red laterite surface which has worn away in successive rainy seasons to cause *fossettes* (dimples) as my chauffeur jokingly termed the holes (*fosses*) that can break an axle if taken awry. Fifteen years after American bombing and the *Khmer Rouge* war bridges are still down in places and detours have to be made over makeshift wooden structures. And 10 years after Pol Pot's grim human levelling, chauffeurs enjoy American-style social equality. In my time as a diplomat in Phnom Penh in the

'50s, my chauffeur would never have let me treat him as my social equal, and it would have been pretentious to have tried to make him do so.

Before embarking on a journey the prudent traveller buys cartons of Heineken—the "in" drink of the affluent—and puts a half dozen cans on ice in the back with him. Beer expresses gratitude on a sweltering, dusty and thirsty road in a way even money cannot. You never know when you may need to distribute such largesse: on the road back from Kompong Som my car broke down and an army jeep stopped to guard us while the chauffeur took the carburettor to bits. On this involuntary halt a whole carton of Heineken scarcely sufficed. On the road between Sisophon and Battambang the Provincial Governor had thoughtfully provided us with a police jeep escort, but after some 20 kilometres the police jeep broke down. As dusk began to fall the police Captain ordered us on to be in Battambang by dark. Our unfortunate guards found some cheer in the carton and a half of Heineken we still had on board. To be on the safe side, I came to reckon on getting through 15 litres of petrol and a carton of beer every 100 kilometres.

On the roads through the more populated areas—such as that from Phnom Penh to the southern fishing port of Kampot—the *Sena Chun* (Home Guard), are much in evidence. They stand by bridges, wander round villages, or sit in sentry posts holding on to the string to raise the red and white pole which divides one stretch of road, one jurisdiction, from the next. They wear such old clothes as are available, but usually they manage to sport at least one item of military attire and carry AK-47s, or some more dated weapon, slung from their shoulders. They are impressive because they are so ubiquitous and because they so evidently take their duty seriously despite their cheery, easy-going Khmer ways. Stories abound of *Sena Chun* peasants shooting dead a single *Khmer Rouge* caught in the act of trying to steal rice or chickens in their search for food which the *Sena Chun* presence denies them.

Night-stops vary with the degree of security. In secure Kampot for instance, the traveller is woken at six with the mesmeric rhythm of Buddhist chants. In Battambang though, he goes to sleep to the hump-backed cacophony of bits of old metal of various sizes being hit every few seconds with iron rods. The town guards are stationed at strategic intervals, and each individual has a makeshift gong to hit after his unseen neighbour in the dark has struck his. The varying notes make a round. This simple expedient tells each man that each individual member of his watch is awake and in position and that all is well. I was told this was a practice thought up by Pol Pot. It is reassuring not only to the guards themselves, but to the traveller, who sleeps the more easily with this futuristic music in his ears.

PART I: HISTORICAL SURVEY

EARLY CAMBODIA

FUNAN AND CHENLA

Khmer myth tells the tale of an Indian Brahmin, Kaundinya, who, in the first century AD, founded the state of Funan, centred in present-day southern Cambodia and the southernmost part of Vietnam. The fourth century accounts of visiting Chinese ambassadors provide the first historical evidence of Funan's existence. Although situated to the south of the Khmer base area in the Champassak area of modern Laos, evidence suggests that members of the Khmer nobility were well placed within the Funanese ruling house; subsequent Khmer dynasties traced their lineage to Funan.

The process of Indianization, which came to shape the politics and culture of subsequent Khmer states, broadened during the fourth and fifth centuries and continued despite the sixth century subjugation of Funan by the rulers of the emerging state of Chenla, situated in modern north-eastern Cambodia. Khmer power, which extended throughout most of the Indo-Chinese region during the seventh century, declined during the eighth century as Chenla was split into rival dominions.

THE ANGKOR EMPIRE

A new Khmer state (Kambu-ja) was established in the early ninth century when a Khmer prince, Jayavarman II, returned from exile or captivity in Java. Jayavarman II, founder of what is conventionally known as the Angkor Empire, established his capital to the north of the *Tonle Sap*. During his reign he firmly established the concept of a unified, independent Khmer state ruled by a *devaraja* (God-King). Indravarman I, a successor of Jayavarman II in the late ninth century, constructed a vast artificial irrigation system which ensured the Kingdom's economic viability.

During the eleventh century, the Angkor Empire reached its apogee under the rule of Suryavarman II, who consolidated Khmer rule over much of modern Cambodia, Thailand and Laos whilst successfully taking his armies into the kingdom of Champa (the modern state of Vietnam) and the Malay peninsular. In addition, Suryavarman commissioned the great temple complex of Angkor Wat, completed at about the time of his death in 1150. Suryavarman's expansive external ambitions, however, combined with the massive construction programmes undertaken during his rule, served to weaken the Angkor Empire. During the mid-twelfth century the resurgent Chams liberated the Champa Kingdom from Khmer domination. A subsequent campaign of attrition against the Khmers culminated in a successful Cham attack against Angkor itself in 1177, precipitating a period of chaos in the Khmer Empire, which was only resolved late in the twelfth century upon the accession of Jayavarman VII. Under his rule, Khmer armies restored and extended the Angkor Empire, again annexing neighbouring Champa.

THE FALL OF ANGKOR

Jayavarman VII was the last of the great Angkor *devarajas*, and following the end of his rule sometime after 1215 the empire went into decline, again losing control of Champa, as well as the Malay peninsula and, forebodingly, northern Thailand. Angkor's loss of territory was accompanied by an abandonment of the Royal Court's adherence to Hinduism and Mahayana Buddhism. In its place, it adopted the Theravada Buddhist belief system of the Tai people located on Angkor's western periphery, in the flourishing state of Sukothai. During the fourteenth century the intricate hydraulic system which had long underpinned Angkor's economic strength was allowed to fall into disrepair, further undermining the empire's capacity for recovery. The eventual conquest of Angkor by Ayutthaya (Sukothai's successor) in 1444 led to the re-establishment of the contracting Khmer kingdom at Phnom Penh, the site of the current capital.

THAI AND VIETNAMESE DOMINANCE

The century and a half following Ayutthaya's capture of Angkor was marked by incessant warfare between the Khmers and the dominant Siamese (Thai). At one point in the late sixteenth century the Khmers were briefly supported by Spanish troops. Eventually, in 1603, Barom Reachea IV was installed in Phnom Penh as a Siamese vassal. A few years later Chey Chetta II, a successor to Barom Reachea, declared Phnom Penh's independence from Siam, supporting his declaration with an assurance of military assistance from the Nguyen dynasty of southern Vietnam. From this point onwards, Cambodia was effectively trapped between two powerful competing states, each of which claimed progressively more Khmer land. By the early nineteenth century competing factions of the Khmer Royal house acknowledged Siamese and Vietnamese suzerainty.

FRENCH RULE

French rule over Cambodia evolved out of her involvement in neighbouring Vietnam. Conquests in Cochin China (southern Vietnam or "Nam Viet") during the 1850s induced the French to expand north-westerly, in order to secure the Mekong against potential aggressors, principally the Thais and the British. In 1863 the French succeeded in pressurizing King Norodom (acceded 1860) into accepting both a protectorate status for his kingdom, and the installation of a French resident-general. Anti-French and anti-monarchical rebellions erupted almost immediately. Two Buddhist monks, Achar Sva and Achar Leak, led unsuccessful insurrections in the mid-1860s. In 1876 a half brother of King Norodom, Si Votha, led a revolt which was eventually put down by French troops.

During the 1870s the French attempted to institute a series of "reforms" in order to modernize the court administration and increase direct control. The French governor of Cochin China and Cambodia, Charles Thomson, attempted to persuade King Norodom to sign a convention introducing the "reforms" in 1884. When the King refused, Thomson summoned troops and gunboats from Saigon, and, eventually, Norodom signed an accord, at gunpoint, which virtually transformed Kampuchea into a full colony. In reaction, significant rebellions broke out in various parts of Cambodia which ended after two years when the French publicly proclaimed their intention to continue to respect Khmer customs and laws. Thereafter, there was little mass opposition to French colonial rule until the independence struggles in the aftermath of World War II.

Whilst other South-East Asian colonies (and even non-colonized Siam) underwent a period of social and political upheaval in the 1920s and 1930s, Cambodia remained a relatively calm and peaceful backwater. Significant political opposition emerged only twice. In 1916, 100,000 peasants marched to Phnom Penh to implore King Sisowath (who had succeeded his half-brother Norodom in 1904) to relieve tax and corvée burdens upon them; nine years later, a French official, Ferdinand Bardez, was assassinated by Khmer peasants whilst collecting taxes in the central province of Kompong Chhnang.

Cambodia's apparent acquiescence in the face of considerable deprivation and exploitation resulted from a number of factors. Unlike Norodom, King Sisowath (1904–27) and his successor and son Monivong (1927–41) both condoned French rule; neither risked a loss of privilege by endorsing anti-colonial sentiment. With the support of the monarchy, France nurtured a non-royal French-orientated élite, which came to serve the colonial power loyally in return for economic privileges. Entry into this élite was regulated by French control of the educational facilities, which were extremely limited. Meanwhile, the countryside remained peaceful, the mass of Khmer peasants living in awe of the monarchy and labouring in conditions of virtual enslavement, as they always had done in some form or another.

The only revolutionary activities in Cambodia during the 1930s were carried out by members of the ethnic Vietnamese and Chinese communities, particularly indentured labourers from northern Vietnam brought to work on Cambodia's eastern rubber plantations. The Vietnam Communist Party and its successor the Indo-China Communist Party (ICP), both of which had been formed in 1930, operated some cells in Cambodia, but ethnic Khmer involvement was limited. A moderate nationalist movement emerged in the late 1930s, inspired by a small circle of Khmer Krom (ethnic Khmer inhabitants of the Mekong delta region of southern Vietnam). The group's leaders were Son Ngoc Thanh and Pach Chhoeun, who had together established the first Khmer-language newspaper, *Nagaravatta* "Angkor Wat", in 1936. Its members travelled around the country's *wats* (Buddhist temples) discreetly disseminating anti-French (and anti-Thai) propaganda.

WORLD WAR II

Following the German invasion of France in 1940, the Japanese served a series of ultimatums upon the French in Indochina. The pro-Vichy French administration capitulated and an agreement was reached in early 1941 whereby local administration and security functions remained in French hands, whereas Japan gained rights of transit through Indochina as well as other military and economic benefits.

In April 1941, following the death of King Monivong, the French authorities placed the 18-year old Prince Norodom Sihanouk on the Cambodian throne, disregarding in the process Monivong's son, Prince Monireth. The French appeared to have been guided by the expectation that the young and inexperienced Sihanouk would be easily manipulated, a calculation that subsequently proved imprudent. The continuation of a form of French rule in Cambodia throughout World War II meant that the effect of the Japanese occupation was less profound than in other South-East Asian countries. Nevertheless, Japan's show of force during the early 1940s emboldened anti-European sentiment, and in July 1942 elements of the Japanese military allegedly approved a coup attempt by Son Ngoc Thanh. France responded by arresting a number of nationalists, prompting demonstrations and riots in Phnom Penh. Thanh escaped to Japan, and other nationalist leaders were captured and imprisoned.

The declining fortunes of the Axis Powers during 1944 fostered insecurity among the Japanese, and in March 1945 they suddenly interned almost all French troops and civil servants in Indochina, offering limited independence to Cambodia, Laos and Vietnam. Pressured by the Japanese, Sihanouk proclaimed Cambodia's independence on March 13, announcing at the same time the formation of a new government composed in the main of members of the pro-French élite. He promulgated a new Basic Law and abrogated all treaties with the French. In May, Son Ngoc Thanh returned to Phnom Penh from Tokyo and was appointed by Sihanouk as Foreign Minister; three months later, just prior to Japan's surrender, a small group of Thanh's supporters stormed the royal palace in Phnom Penh, and effectively forced Sihanouk to appoint Thanh as Prime Minister. Thanh remained in the post for less than two months before being removed by Allied troops arriving in Cambodia to disarm the Japanese and re-establish French authority. He was arrested and ordered into exile, first in Saigon and later in France.

PRE-INDEPENDENCE POLITICS AND THE ISSARAK STRUGGLE

Commitments made by the Free French during the War made it incumbent upon them to offer some concessions towards independence upon their return in late 1945. Hence, Cambodia's protectorate relationship was abolished, and it became an autonomous state within the French Union. Shortly after, the Khmer Issarak movement, which was first established in Thailand in the early 1940s, began eight years of armed resistance to the French. In September 1946, nationwide elections were held for a 67-member Constituent Assembly to approve a draft constitution which had been formulated earlier by a joint

Franco-Khmer commission. The pro-Thanh Democratic Party led by Prince Sisowath Youtevong (who died in mid-1947) took 50 of the seats, with another 14 going to the pro-monarchist Liberal Party and the remainder to independents. The Democrat-dominated Assembly made some revisions to the draft constitution, which was eventually approved by Sihanouk in July 1947. The Constitution provided for regular multi-party elections, and a Cabinet responsible to a National Assembly; the King was obliged to use his power in conformity with the new Constitution. In December 1947 elections were held for the new National Assembly, and the Democrats achieved a comfortable majority.

Although by far the most popular party, Democrat support for Son Ngoc Thanh and the Khmer Issarak movement brought them into conflict with Sihanouk and the French. Eventually, in September 1949, Sihanouk dissolved the Assembly and formed a new government around a group of conservative ex-Democrats. Nevertheless, political stability remained elusive and at least six Cabinets were formed during the two-year period following the Assembly's dissolution.

Increasing Issarak activity during 1950 brought into question Sihanouk's plan to hold a general election in late 1951. As the war between the French and the Viet Minh had intensified during the late 1940s, the turmoil had spread into Cambodia. The French, through Sihanouk, had recruited Cambodians to fight against the Viet Minh; at the same time, the Viet Minh had encouraged anti-French nationalist sentiment among the Khmer. In this environment the Khmer Issaraks emerged to conduct a guerrilla war against the French and Sihanouk. As the military situation veered in favour of the Viet Minh, so their Issarak allies increased their activities and by the early 1950s they were over 5,000 strong and in control of large areas of the countryside. The dominant, rural-based Issarak wing led by Son Ngoc Minh was strongly pro-Viet Minh, whereas a weaker urban-based strand, led by, amongst others, Son Ngoc Thanh, Dap Chhuon and Prince Norodom Chantaraingsey, was largely anti-communist and wary of the Vietnamese.

In April 1950, the pro-Viet Minh Issaraks congregated in south-west Cambodia and established a United Issarak Front (UIF). Two months later, Son Ngoc Minh, the UIF leader and head of a communist Issarak proto-government, declared Cambodia's "independence", claiming control of at least one third of Cambodian territory. During 1951 the pro-Viet Minh Issaraks formed the country's first communist party (the Khmer People's Revolutionary Party—KPRP) after the Indo-Chinese Communist Party had agreed to dissolve itself into three national parties for Vietnam, Laos and Cambodia. Meanwhile, in the early 1950s, another revolutionary current was developing among Khmer students studying in Paris, who had formed a "Marxist Circle". Several members of this group, including Saloth Sar (Pol Pot) and Ieng Sary, returned to Cambodia in 1953 to join Khmer and Vietnamese communist fighters in eastern Cambodia.

INDEPENDENCE

Despite the mounting Issarak threat, national elections went ahead in September 1951, with the Democrats again winning a large majority. Other parties which gained representation included right-wing groups such as Lon Nol's "Khmer Renovation" and former Issarak leader Dap Chhuon's "Victorious North-East".

Following their victory, the Democrats came under increasing pressure from the French and the right-wing parties over their alleged Issarak sympathies. In June 1952 leaflets were distributed in Phnom Penh, signed by Dap Chhuon, calling upon Sihanouk to dismiss the Democrat government. In response, the Democrats rounded up a number of rightists for questioning, provoking an opposition outcry. In these circumstances, Sihanouk dismissed the government and unsuccessfully beseeched the Assembly to allow him to assume personal leadership, guaranteeing full independence by 1955. In January 1953 he went ahead and abolished the Assembly and effectively introduced martial law, thereby firmly aligning himself with Lon Nol and the leading rightists. Large numbers of Democrats were arrested, accused of following the orders of the Issarak and the Viet Minh.

In February 1953 Sihanouk embarked on his "Royal Crusade for Independence". He visited a number of Western capitals pressing his demands, which were initially rejected by the French. In June he established a government in internal exile in Siemreap. The French, facing an increasingly stiff military test in Vietnam and Laos, and concerned about the possible drift away from the conservative throne to the Viet Minh-associated left, eventually made a number of concessions leading to the declaration of Cambodian independence on Nov. 9, 1953.

THE GENEVA CONFERENCE—INTRODUCTION OF THE SANGKUM SYSTEM

The Indochinese phase of the Geneva Conference held between May and July 1954 represented a massive achievement for Sihanouk, with his Royal government being accorded international recognition as the sole legitimate authority within Cambodia. Unlike the revolutionaries in Vietnam and Laos, the Cambodian Issarak were accorded no representation at the conference and were not allotted regroupment areas, leading to subsequent accusations among Cambodian communists that they had been "betrayed" by China or the Viet-Minh. Under the terms of the Geneva Agreements, Sihanouk pledged to institute a free and open political system, to be demonstrated through the holding of internationally supervised elections in 1955.

Sihanouk's success at Geneva, coupled with the promise of free elections, left the Cambodian revolutionary forces with little choice but to lay down their arms and enter the political process or to withdraw to North Vietnam. About 1,000 communists, including Son Ngoc Minh, chose the latter option, whilst the remainder of the pro-Viet Minh Issarak, led by such figures as Keo Meas, Non Suon and Pen Yuth, returned from "liberated" regions of the countryside to Phnom Penh where they founded the *Krom Pracheachon* (Citizens' Group). At the same time, the non-Viet Minh Issarak (the Thanhists) founded the Khmer Independence Party, while a more radical version of the Democrat Party emerged, many of its leading figures drawn from the Paris "Marxist Circle" group.

The re-organization of the legitimate left ahead of the elections forced the right into realignment. In late 1954, Lon Nol and Dap Chhuon formed a "rightist, monarchist and traditionalist" coalition which broke up in February 1955, most of its membership joining the *Sangkum Reastr Niyum* (Popular Socialist Community), an organization formed that month by Sihanouk. On March 2, in order to avoid constitutional constraints on his political actions, Sihanouk abdicated in favour of his father, Norodom Suramarit. The new King died in April 1960, but Sihanouk successfully averted a political crisis by taking the position of head of state without re-ascending the throne.

Following an election campaign characterized by widespread harassment of the opposition, the *Sangkum* won a massive victory in September 1955. The International Control Commission certified the election as "correct", but there were widespread reports alleging fraud and voter intimidation. The official results gave *Sangkum* all 91 National Assembly seats, with 82 per cent of the vote. The Democrats gained 12 per cent and *Pracheachon* 4 per cent. The *Sangkum* repeated this performance in the elections of 1958, 1962 and 1966.

THE LOST NEUTRALITY

SITTING ON THE FENCE, 1955–70

Having gained control of Cambodia's internal political machinery through the *Sangkum* victory of September 1955, Prince Sihanouk's most pressing task was to prevent his country becoming entangled in the war brewing in neighbouring Vietnam and Laos. Before the 1955 elections, Sihanouk had clearly indicated his intention to attempt to navigate a path through the conflict by adopting a neutralist foreign policy.

At the Bandung conference in April 1955 Sihanouk gave private assurances to China and North Vietnam that Cambodia would not succumb to pressure to join the USA's recently created vehicle of containment, the South-East Asia Treaty Organization (SEATO). The next month, however, the Prince signed a military aid agreement with the USA, a move which aggravated both Hanoi and Beijing. Just as the scales appeared to be tilting towards the USA in early 1956, he paid a visit to Beijing. Subsequently, Cambodia became the recipient of China's first-ever aid grant to a non-communist country. In response, South Vietnam and Thailand briefly imposed an economic embargo against Phnom Penh. Eventually in mid-1958, Sihanouk established diplomatic relations with Beijing, although he refrained from formalizing his country's links with Hanoi.

The internal repercussions of Cambodia's neutralist stance were highly beneficial for Sihanouk and the *Sangkum*. By not capitulating to US pressure, the Prince improved his standing among the urban left, large elements of which he had previously alienated by his use of fraud and intimidation at the 1955 elections. As a consequence of this, the left-wing *Pracheachon* even offered to enter into a coalition government with the *Sangkum*,[1] at a *Sangkum* conference held in April 1956. Meanwhile, the *Sangkum* system had firm support in the countryside, where the highly traditional peasantry had responded positively to Sihanouk's portrayal of himself as the nation's "provider" and protector of Buddhism.

The *Sangkum* won another overwhelming victory in National Assembly elections held in 1958. Alone amongst the opposition, *Pracheachon* fielded five candidates. However, Sihanouk personally selected all *Sangkum* candidates (one for each of the 62 constituencies), among them a small number of young, left-wing French-trained intellectuals. After the elections, Sihanouk embarked on a fresh experiment, bringing some of these intellectuals into the Cabinet and other positions of responsibility. Notable amongst those incorporated into the *Sangkum* system in this way were Hou Youn, Hu Nim and Chau Seng. Sihanouk continued with this experiment until 1962, although he always took care never to allow any of the intellectuals to develop independent political power bases and, as Vickery has pointed out, political and economic power throughout this period "remained solidly in the hands of the old Right".[2]

During the late 1950s the left used their new-found position of influence to call for Cambodian support for the Communists fighting the repressive Diem regime in neighbouring South Vietnam. Sihanouk's ambiguous relationship with the left-wing elements within his government meant that neither the USA nor the Cambodian right could guess the Prince's intentions. However, he appeared to harden his anti-USA stance following a large-scale intrusion into Cambodia by South Vietnamese troops in mid-1958. The incursion was apparently carried out in an attempt to provoke Sihanouk into adopting a more pro-American position. The action conspicuously failed to do this, and according to some sources,[3] Sihanouk's irritation at the incursion provoked the CIA into starting preparations for his overthrow.

The Prince's anti-Americanism, and the pro-National Liberation Front rhetoric of the *Sangkum* left, motivated rightist elements to become more voluble. Just before National Assembly elections in June 1962, almost the entire *Pracheachon* leadership were arrested, and following student demonstrations in Siem Reap in early 1963, Sihanouk was obliged to abandon his sponsorship

[1]Kiernan, Ben. *How Pol Pot Came to Power*, London 1985, p. 170.
[2]Vickery, Michael. 'Looking Back at Cambodia, 1942–76' in Kiernan, Ben and Boua, Chanthou, eds., *Peasants and Politics in Kampuchea 1942–81*, London 1982, p. 100.
[3]For Example, Blum, William. *The CIA: A Forgotten History*, London 1986, p. 149.

of the intellectual left. Khieu Samphan and Hou Youn were forced to resign from the Cabinet, although both remained in Phnom Penh unlike Pol Pot, Ieng Sary and Son Senn of the "Paris Circle" group who disappeared from the capital in mid-1963 at the height of the anti-left repression.

Ironically, as the left came under attack, Cambodia entered its so-called "*Sangkum* Socialist" period. In late 1963, import-export trade and banks were nationalized and a few months later Sihanouk discontinued all US aid projects. Eventually, in May 1965 diplomatic relations with the USA were ended. According to Vickery the anti-American path taken by Sihanouk and his supporters in the traditional élite during the early and mid-1960s was based on an assessment that "the USA would give up (in Vietnam) and the National Liberation Front (NLF or Vietcong) would win".[4]

The termination of US aid forced the Cambodian élite to extract greater profits from the peasantry and this in turn led to growing anti-government sentiment in the countryside. This period of rising tension coincided with fresh elections in late 1966 and the subsequent appointment of a right-wing government led by Gen. Lon Nol. In early 1967 a peasant rebellion erupted in Samlaut in north-western Cambodia and within a matter of months had developed into a full-scale rural revolt, with Cambodian communists led by Pol Pot (dubbed the *Khmers Rouges* by Sihanouk) playing a leading role. Lon Nol's attempt to suppress the rebellion by brute force met with only partial success, and in April he was forced to resign the Premiership. Meanwhile, Sihanouk's alarm over the revolt acted as a warning to the former *Sangkum* leftists, and by October Khieu Samphan, Hou Youn and Hu Nim had all disappeared. At the time, the three were presumed to have been murdered.

By 1967 US military operations in South Vietnam had pushed an increasing number of communist guerrillas across the border into Cambodian "sanctuaries". After the decimation of the NLF forces during the Tet offensive in early 1968, the Cambodian sanctuaries took on an even greater importance for the Vietnamese revolution and in March 1969 the USA began to secretly bomb them. The US escalation of the Vietnam War and the accompanying communist infringements into eastern Cambodia led Sihanouk to reassess the overall situation. In mid-1969 he re-established diplomatic relations with the USA, at the same time recognizing the NLF's Provisional Revolutionary Government.

[4]Kiernan and Boua. op. cit. p. 105.

THE *COUP*

Sihanouk has always maintained that the CIA organized his removal in early 1970. However, it seems unlikely that a high-level decision would have been taken to topple Sihanouk at a time when the Prince was shifting perceptively towards the USA. Nevertheless, circumstances and testimony indicate a certain amount of "low-level" US complicity, and it seems highly unlikely that Nixon and Kissinger's assertions of surprise and dismay over the Prince's downfall were genuine. So, the *coup* was primarily an internal affair, arising out of conflict among Cambodian élites.[5] According to Vickery,[6] the economic "reforms" introduced by Sihanouk in 1963 had turned over the direction of the economy to a group associated specifically with the Prince, at the expense of another right-wing faction. It was the leading members of the latter faction, "the big guns of the Cambodian right"[7] including Sirik Matak (Sihanouk's cousin) and Gen. Lon Nol, who had most to gain from the Prince's downfall.

Lon Nol resumed the premiership in August 1969. The formation by him of an overtly right-wing government marked a weakening in Sihanouk's personal authority, as was shown by the wide-ranging conditions which the General laid down for accepting office. Sihanouk travelled to France for one of his periodic rest–cures in early January 1970, planning to return via Moscow and Beijing. However, on March 8, whilst Sihanouk was still in Paris, anti-NLF protests erupted in Svay Rieng province, a border area particularly affected by infiltration and bombing. Three days later, large crowds of demonstrators congregated outside the North Vietnamese and PRG embassies in Phnom Penh. The mob sacked both embassies before marching on the city's Vietnamese quarter, where a number of Catholic churches were burned down. In a telegram from Paris, Sihanouk alleged that the attacks on the embassies had been organized by "personalities aiming . . . . to throw our country into the arms of an imperialist capitalist power", and announced his intention to return to Cambodia. However, instead of returning immediately to Phnom Penh, Sihanouk left Paris on March 13 for Moscow. That day, Lon Nol issued an ultimatum demanding that all NLF and North Vietnamese troops should be withdrawn from Cambodia by dawn on March 15.

The police, acting on the orders of Sihanouk loyalists in the Cabinet, made an attempt to arrest Lon Nol during the night of March 16–17. The attempt

[5]Vickery, Michael. *Kampuchea: Politics, Economics and Society*. London, 1986. p. 20.
[6]Vickery, Michael. *Looking Back at Cambodia, 1942–76*. In Kiernan and Boua. 1982. p. 108.
[7]ibid.

failed and on March 18 troops took up positions outside the city's main points, closed the airport down and cut off telephone communications with the outside world. A joint session of the National Assembly and Royal Council was convened, during which several deputies violently denounced Sihanouk and his wife Monique. Eventually, in the early afternoon, a motion withdrawing the Assembly's confidence in the Prince was put to the vote and was officially stated to have been adopted by 92 votes to nil. The next day the National Assembly declared a state of emergency and granted Lon Nol full powers. The US government announced that Sihanouk had been legally deposed and that the issue of recognition for the new regime "does not arise". Cheng Heng took the oath of office as head of state on March 21. Finally, in October, Lon Nol abolished the monarchy and declared the Khmer Republic.

Sihanouk was informed of his deposition on March 18, shortly before he left Moscow for Beijing. On March 21, after consultations with Zhou Enlai and Pham Van Dong (the North Vietnamese premier) the Prince began to draw up a programme of co-ordinated resistance to Lon Nol, and his plans were reportedly secretly passed by the Chinese to Pol Pot (who was also in Beijing) for approval.[8] On March 23 Sihanouk announced the formation of a National United Front of Kampuchea (NUFK) to liberate the country from the "dictatorship and oppression of the clique of traitorous and pro-imperialist reactionaries". The next day, Sihanouk issued a communiqué calling on his supporters inside Cambodia to take up arms against Lon Nol.

In Phnom Penh, Sihanouk's March 24 invitation to revolt fell on deaf ears. The Lon Nol-Sirik Matak *coup* had been greeted with some relief in the capital, especially among the middle class who approved of the new regime's plans for economic regeneration. However, two days after Sihanouk's call for an uprising there was an almost spontaneous outburst of rural unrest which lasted for three or four days. The mass demonstrations took place in towns such as Kompong Cham, Siem Reap and Takeo and were overtly pro-Sihanouk, although the new government spoke of "Vietcong incitement". The unrest was brutally suppressed by the Army, and hundreds of peasants were killed and thousands arrested. To counteract the royalist demonstrations, the government launched a campaign to rally support among the students and the intelligentsia. Large numbers of political prisoners were released and a "Committee of Intellectuals" established to investigate the possibility of establishing a republic.

[8]Kiernan, Ben. 1985. op. cit. p. 298.

INVASION

The Lon Nol–Sirik Matak *coup* shattered the illusion of Cambodian neutrality and allowed the full effects of the Vietnam War to be felt in Cambodia. During his last months in power, Sihanouk had moved closer to the USA, but he had never cast off completely his cloak of neutrality, a concept he had consistently equated with Cambodia's survival. However, the overtly pro-USA orientations of the right-wing *coup* plotters were clear even before they had officially overthrown the Prince. Lon Nol had invited South Vietnamese troops to begin shelling communist sanctuaries on March 16, a full two days before Sihanouk was officially deposed. On March 20, South Vietnamese troops had entered Cambodia in force. They were accompanied by ethnic Khmer troops (Khmers of Kampuchea Krom—KKK) and US "Green Beret" advisers. These incursions continued and, in response, the Vietnamese communists were forced to move deeper into eastern and southern Cambodia. The feeble Cambodian Army, powerless to prevent the communist manoeuvres, took their revenge on Vietnamese civilians. The first massacre occurred at Prasot on April 9–10 and then between April 12–17 the bodies of several hundred men and boys were seen floating down the Mekong at Neak Luong; many had their hands tied and had bullet wounds in their heads and necks, whilst others were headless.

In a personal letter to US President Nixon on April 20, Lon Nol made an urgent appeal for US military aid. By this time the US military command had started preparations for a full-scale incursion into Cambodia. The offensive began on April 29 when a 12,000-strong South Vietnamese force entered the "Parrot's Beak" area of Svay Rieng province. On May 1 a joint US–South Vietnamese force launched an offensive directed against the salient of Kompong Cham province known as the "Fish Hook", which projects into South Vietnamese territory. Before the attack waves of B-52 bombers dropped hundreds of tons of bombs on the area and fighter-bombers carried out a massive number of tactical air strikes. About 8,000 US troops took part in the attack, the largest US offensive in Indochina since 1968. The US–South Vietnamese troops remained in Cambodia until late June.

As part of his "Vietnamization" policy President Nixon had announced on April 20 that some 150,000 US troops were to be withdrawn from Vietnam during the next twelve months. In a speech to the nation on May 1, Nixon used the planned withdrawal as justification for the Cambodian incursion, claiming that the continued existence of communist sanctuaries in Cambodia constituted "an unacceptable risk" to those troops remaining after the partial withdrawal. Nixon was also apparently convinced, despite receiving advice to the contrary, that the invasion would destroy the Vietnamese Communist headquarters (COSVN).

In actual fact, the invasion achieved nothing of the sort. For the most part, the Vietnamese communists simply avoided confrontation with the invading troops, repositioning themselves further westward into the Cambodian interior. Villages were ravaged, civilians uprooted and killed and a large amount of communist supplies captured, but COSVN was never found, let alone destroyed. The brutality of the invaders only served to further radicalize the rural Cambodian population. In the United States, the invasion prompted a vast outcry of protest with four students being shot dead by the National Guard at Kent State University. The action also provoked high-level resignations from Kissinger's National Security Council. Eventually, in December, the Cooper–Church amendment to the US Foreign Military Sales Bill was passed forbidding the sending of US troops or military advisers to Cambodia. In Phnom Penh, the invasion caught Lon Nol unawares and he described the action as a violation of Cambodia's territorial integrity.

Meanwhile the invasion demonstrated to the Chinese that their diplomatic efforts (underway since the March *coup*) to persuade Lon Nol to allow the Democratic Republic of Vietnam (DRV, North Vietnam) and NLF sanctuaries to remain intact had been ineffectual. Hence, on May 5, Sihanouk announced the formation of a government-in-exile, the Royal Government of National Union of Kampuchea (RGNUK), which was immediately recognized by both China and North Vietnam. Included in the government were the former Sangkum leftists, Khieu Samphan, Hou Youn and Hu Nim, but not, initially, any representatives of the "Paris Circle" group who had disappeared in 1963.

CIVIL WAR

Following the US invasion, the war in Cambodia soon settled into a pattern. The Republican forces (Lon Nol's troops supported by South Vietnamese units) held the towns while the revolutionary forces (*Khmers Rouges* and Sihanoukist troops supported by both DRV and NLF units) controlled the countryside. The latter generally launched offensives during the dry season (January–June) and each year they captured more territory. They quickly succeeded in isolating Phnom Penh by launching attacks on the capital's road, rail and river communications. The Republican forces suffered a particularly severe defeat in late 1971 during an attempt to relieve the town of Kompong Thom in central Cambodia. Codenamed Chenla II, the operation started in August

1971 and by October the Republican forces appeared to have won a great victory, having travelled up Highway 6 before successfully relieving Kompong Thom which had been encircled by communists since June 1970. However, the communist counter-offensives in October and November succeeded in cutting the Republican forces in two, and restored the position before Chenla II began. The Republican losses were great and the defeat did much to lower the morale of Lon Nol's forces.

The revolutionary forces greatly extended their control over Cambodia during 1972. In the east, where the DRV forces mainly operated, they held virtually the entire area between the South Vietnamese border and the Mekong, and in the south they overran much of Kampot and Takeo provinces. In the north and west the Republican forces held only isolated pockets around a few towns and Phnom Penh itself was periodically subjected to bombardment and commando raids. The US magazine *Newsweek* estimated in August that the revolutionaries controlled over 80 per cent of the area of the country and half the population.

As the military situation deteriorated, the urban population and the Army became increasingly disillusioned with the Lon Nol regime. Inflation was a major problem for the government. The war had greatly reduced production of rice and rubber, the country's chief exports. The main rice-growing areas were almost wholly controlled by the NUFK and communications between Kompong Som, the only seaport, and Phnom Penh were invariably cut by guerrilla attacks.

Lon Nol responded to the growing unrest by assuming increasingly personal political powers. In October 1971 the National Assembly (which had last been elected in 1966) was deprived of its legislative powers and was transformed into a "Constituent Assembly". A state of emergency was declared a few days later and Lon Nol announced that the government would rule by decree. In a radio broadcast he asserted that the government had decided not to "vainly play the game of democracy and freedom", which, he claimed, would only lead to "complete defeat". In March 1972, the Constituent Assembly itself was dissolved and a few days later Lon Nol announced that he had assumed the titles of President of the Republic and President of the Council of Ministers. He soon appointed Son Ngoc Thanh as Prime Minister. Thanh had returned to Phnom Penh in 1970 after the *coup* and had worked as an adviser to Lon Nol. Operating with the South Vietnamese and Thai governments and the CIA, he had played an important role in organizing the Khmer community in Vietnam into an anti-communist force.

Lon Nol was formally elected as President in June in the country's first presidential election. Three months later, National Assembly elections were held in Republican-controlled areas; predictably, the Social Republican Party (SRP) led by Lon Nol's brother, Col. Lon Non, won all 126 seats. Thanh was forced to resign as Prime Minister in October and was replaced by Hang Thun Hak, a SRP member and former *Pracheachon* supporter. After only six months in office Hak was discarded by Lon Nol in an attempt by the President to broaden the basis of the Republican regime. A Supreme State Council was established in late April 1973 consisting of the three main opposition leaders. The National Assembly was suspended for six months and a new Cabinet headed by In Tam was formed in mid-May.

THE 1973 BOMBING

In late January 1973 the Paris Agreements on "ending the war and restoring peace in Vietnam" were signed by the opposing sides. The Agreements contained no detailed references to Cambodia or Laos, but in the aftermath of the signing there was a brief respite as attempts were made to try and forge a ceasefire. The NUFK rejected the offer of entering into peace talks with the Lon Nol regime and in early February issued a communiqué insisting that the fight was to continue. The *Khmers Rouges* subsequently explained their decision not to enter into negotiations in terms of their apprehension over Vietnamese plans to subvert the Cambodian revolution. Whatever the reason, the NUFK's announcement of renewed hostilities motivated the USA to embark on a massived bombing campaign over Cambodia.

US bombing attacks on Cambodia had been in progress since March 1969. For the first 14 months B-52 bombers made 3,630 secret raids against suspected communist sanctuaries at a time when the Nixon administration claimed to be respecting Cambodian neutrality.[9] Official US records were falsified to conceal the bombings from Congress and the so-called "Menu" missions were not disclosed until July 1973. When the truth was revealed Nixon and Kissinger both maintained that secrecy had been necessary to protect Sihanouk who, they claimed, had encouraged the raids. The bombing continued after the May 1970 invasion, and was mostly concentrated in the Eastern provinces. The attacks killed an unknown number of innocent civilians and aggravated the already serious refugee problem. In all of 1972, US B-52s and fighter bombers dropped over 53,000 tons of bombs onto Cambodia. However, between February and August 1973 the total was 257,000 tons, dropped over almost all regions of

[9]Shawcross, William. *Sideshow: Kissinger, Nixon and the Destruction of Cambodia*. London, 1979. p. 28.

the country. The bombing, and with it official American military operations in Indochina, ended on Aug. 15 after Congress had earlier blocked the use of funds for the continued air war. A week before the final bombing mission, an off-target B-52 dropped its entire load on the Republican-held ferry town of Neak Luong, killing 56 soldiers and 81 civilians.

The 1973 bombardment was certainly successful in preventing the revolutionary forces from launching an immediate, and almost certainly successful, assault on Phnom Penh. However, as Kiernan[10] has pointed out, if the revolutionary forces had been allowed to overthrow Lon Nol in 1973, then the Cambodian people might well have been spared the excesses of the *Khmer Rouge* regime of 1975–79. In the immediate aftermath of the January 1973 Paris Agreements, the *Khmers Rouges* were easily the dominant faction in the Cambodian revolutionary forces. In most regions, Sihanoukists and NLF/DRV fighters had been isolated and purges of pro-Vietnamese cadres were underway. However, within the *Khmer Rouge* ranks, no one faction was in complete control, although the ultra-nationalist Pol Pot clique was certainly in a stronger position than its relatively moderate rivals. The bombing gave the Pol Pot group a political leverage within the revolution which it might never have gained otherwise.[11] A disproportionate number of "moderates" died in the bombing and were replaced by new recruits brutalized by the assault. As William Shawcross has described it "these peasant boys and girls, clad in black, moving slowly through the mud, half-crazed with terror [were] urged on by their commanders, a small group of hardened zealous men who had lived up to 10 years in the isolation of the jungles, whose only experience of alliance was betrayal, whose only knowledge of war was massive retaliation".[12] Shawcross continues:

"For these men, 1973 confirmed a historic conviction that survival, let alone victory, could be guaranteed only by absolute independence and an astonishing fixity of purpose. They faced an enemy who at least appeared to have enormous support from his sponsor, while they themselves could not trust even their own leader, let alone their friends. Their attack upon Phnom Penh was a madness born of desperate isolation, which bred a dreadful hatred of the enemy and a contempt for the attitudes of the outside world".

[10]ibid. pp. 390–93.
[11]Kiernan and Boua. op. cit. p. 282.
[12]Shawcross. op. cit. pp. 298–99.

KHMER ROUGE VICTORY

The *Khmers Rouges* maintained their pressure on Phnom Penh during 1973, subjecting the capital to an almost constant blockade and frequent bombardment. The economy was in a state of disarray, with spiralling inflation, food shortages and constant strikes and stoppages. The political situation was equally chaotic, with another change of government in late 1973 when Long Boret replaced In Tam as Prime Minister. During 1974 the military situation was in stalemate with Phnom Penh still isolated. The Republican army was able to hold its own largely because of the superiority of its equipment. The *Khmers Rouges* received only comparatively small amounts of military aid from China, North Vietnam and North Korea.

At the beginning of January 1975 the *Khmers Rouges* won a major victory when they seized control of almost the entire length of the Mekong and were able to halt supplies entering Phnom Penh. At the same time, they attacked the outskirts of Phnom itself, and over the next three months they made steady advances, while the Republican forces experienced supply difficulties not only along the Mekong but also by air. The revolutionary forces began to break through republican lines on the capital's outskirts during March. Embassies started to evacuate their staff and republican leaders began to escape into exile, among them Lon Nol who flew to Hawaii on April 1. In accordance with the republican constitution, the President of the Senate, Maj.-Gen. Saukham Khoy, assumed the position of interim President. On April 12, Khoy also left the country along with all the Americans in Phnom Penh. At daybreak on April 17, the *Khmers Rouges* launched its final attack, and by early afternoon the Republican army had formally surrendered.

POL POT IN POWER

CONSOLIDATION

The new government officially displayed to the world after April 17, 1975, was a variation of the exiled, Sihanoukist-dominated government established in 1970. In actual fact, most of the ministers remained in Beijing, along with Sihanouk, the new official head of state. The government was little more than a camouflage, masking deep divisions within the Cambodian revolution.

According to Michael Vickery,[1] there were two discernible opposing factions, separated by the length of their association with Sihanouk during the 1960s. The first group, composed of Hu Nim, Hou Youn, Khieu Samphan, Poc Deuskoma and Tiv Ol had been associated with the Prince's *Sangkum* experiment, and had held out until 1967 before absconding to the countryside. The leading members of the second faction had abandoned Sihanouk earlier, in 1963, and included Saloth Sar (Pol Pot), Ieng Sary, Son Sen, Nuon Chea, Koy Thoun and the two sisters, Khieu Thirith (Sary's wife) and Khieu Ponnary (Sar's wife).

With hindsight, divisions within the new leadership could be detected at the time of the fall of the republican regime. According to Ben Kiernan[2] the first policy decision of the new regime, the evacuation of Phnom Penh, was largely motivated by political ambitions, constituting "an important move in the Pol Pot group's bid for total control of the revolution".

[1]Vickery, Michael. *Cambodia: 1975–1982*, Boston 1984, pp. 145–146.
[2]Kiernan, Ben. 'Pol Pot and the Kampuchean Communist Movement' in Ben Kiernan and Chanthou Boua, eds., *Peasants and Politics in Kampuchea 1942–81*, London 1982, p. 286.

Battalions of bedraggled *Khmers Rouges* fighters led by independent military commanders entered Phnom Penh on April 17. Each commander occupied a different sector of the city. Within hours, they were ordering the civilian population to leave for the countryside, warning that the city was about to be attacked by US agents. Evidence suggests that some commanders (possibly from the Eastern Zone) did not wholly approve of the evacuation and carried out their orders with a measure of uncertainty; other sectors, possibly under the control of Northern Zone commanders, were emptied with brutal efficiency. There were some reports of fighting in the city between northern and eastern troops.

During the remainder of 1975, the Pol Pot group strengthened their position but did not attain complete dominance. In July, the armed forces were unified, probably under the command of Son Sen. The next month Son Sen and Ieng Sary were appointed to leading positions within the Council of Ministers. During the same month, Hou Yuon, Minister of the Interior, Co-operatives and Communal Reforms, was probably arrested and executed.

A new Constitution (the country's third, following those of Sihanouk's monarchy and Lon Nol's Khmer Republic) came into force in January 1976. The country was officially renamed Democratic Kampuchea (DK) and elections were held to a newly created 250-seat National Assembly in March.

Sihanouk, who had only returned to Phnom Penh in September 1975, resigned as head of state in early April 1976. He informed the government that all his wishes had been realized and that he was now enjoying "happiness beyond my imagination". In actual fact, the Prince was then placed under virtual house arrest. Later that month, Pen Nouth announced his resignation as Premier and a new government structure was disclosed. Khieu Samphan was appointed President of the State Presidium, with So Phim and Nhim Ros as first and second Vice-Presidents respectively. Noun Chea became head of the National Assembly standing committee.

Pol Pot was appointed as Prime Minister, at the head of a government which also included as new members Yun Yat (the wife of Son Sen) and Vorn Vet. The other members included Son Sen, Hou Nim, Thiounn Thioeunn, Ieng Thirith and Toch Phoeun. It was at this point that Saloth Sar adopted the name Pol Pot. This caused confusion amongst most Western observers, who were surprised at what appeared to be the promotion of a complete unknown.

Despite Pol Pot's appointment as Premier, the April 1976 remodelling of the government structure was not necessarily wholly to the advantage of his coterie. In fact, Ieng Sary made the staggering assertion two years later that the April changes had constituted an attempted *coup* by "Vietnamese and KGB agents". Sary was most probably referring to the appointment of So Phim and Nhim Ros to the State Presidium. Phim and Ros were both members of the previously unrepresented clique of veteran revolutionaries, associates of which had either fled to Vietnam with Son Ngoc Minh in 1954 or had remained in Phnom Penh to form the *Pracheachon* Party. As such they represented a pro-Hanoi counterweight to Pol Pot's power-base in the Cabinet.

During the next few months a frenzied struggle developed between the Pol Pot clique and the supporters of a more pro-Vietnamese line. Kiernan[3] provides evidence of significant shifts in domestic and foreign policies during this period and also explores what he perceives as causal linkages between domestic upheavals in China and internal Cambodian affairs. Eventually, on Sept. 27, Phnom Penh radio announced that Pol Pot had resigned the premiership for "health reasons". He was replaced in an acting capacity by Nuon Chea.

Within a month, although it was never officially announced, Pol Pot was back as Prime Minister. Having secured the support of at least two powerful zonal military commanders (Ta Mok of the south-west and Pok of the north), he went to war against rival pro-Vietnamese zonal armies and their supporters in the central administration. Over the next two years a large number of Pol Pot's opponents were physically eliminated [see list below], after first confessing their "crimes" at the infamous Tuol Sleng interrogation camp in Phnom Penh.

The arrest and execution in January 1977 of Koy Thuon, Minister of Commerce and Communist Party secretary of the Northern Zone, heralded the start of extensive provincial purges. Large numbers of northern cadres were executed and replaced by Pol Pot loyalists from Ta Mok's South-West Zone. From mid-1977 the purges widened in scope, and some areas underwent the ordeal twice, with the beneficiaries of the first purge themselves being eradicated.

In late September 1977 Pol Pot delivered a long speech in Phnom Penh in which he publicly revealed for the first time that the Communist Party of Cambodia (CPC) had controlled the country since April 1975 and that he was the party general secretary. Prior to this the party had been known to the population only as *Angkar* (the Organization). In his speech, Pol Pot claimed that a "handful of reactionary elements", constituting, at the most, 2 per cent of the Cambodian population, were carrying out subversive activities. They

[3]ibid. pp. 293–294.

had to be dealt with by "separating, educating and co-opting elements that can be won over and corrected to the people's side, neutralizing any reluctant elements so that they will not undermine the revolution, and isolating and eradicating only the smallest possible number of the elements who are cruel and who determinedly oppose the revolution".

Amongst those "determinedly opposing the revolution" at the time of Pol Pot's public emergence was So Phim, First Vice-President of the State Presidium and party secretary of the Eastern Zone. Phim appeared to have a considerable power-base in the Eastern Zone and he apparently refused Pol Pot's demands to initiate purges. Eventually, in May 1978 South-Western troops under the command of Ta Mok and Son Sen launched a full-scale attack against the Eastern Zone dissidents. The attack succeeded, Phim committed suicide and his forces collapsed. The invading Pol Pot loyalists proceeded to exact a terrible revenge for Phim's obduracy, massacring thousands of peasants deemed disloyal. Others were forcibly deported to be tortured and executed in other zones. Many survivors escaped into Vietnam, among them the nucleus of the People's Republic of Kampuchea (PRK) government established with the help of Vietnamese forces in early 1979 [see below].

With the death of So Phim and the crushing of the Eastern Zone, Pol Pot had won his battle against the "internal reactionaries". Further liquidations followed, most notably the "suicide" of Vorn Vet in November 1978, but, through the application of the crudest of political tactics, the Pol Pot clique managed to gain absolute control of the party and government. By mid-1978 this clique consisted, in essence, of three married couples (Pol Pot and Khieu Ponnary; Ieng Sary and Khieu Thirith; and Son Sen and Yun Yat), a few trusted lieutenants (Ta Mok and Nuon Chea) and a smaller number of lucky survivors (among them Khieu Samphan).

Principal casualties of Pol Pot's purges, 1976–1978

Non Suon, Minister of Agriculture, executed November 1976.
Koy Thuon, Minister of Commerce, executed January 1977.
Touch Phoeun, Minister of Public Works, executed January 1977.
Sua Doeum, Minister of Trade, executed February 1977.
Hou Nim, Minister of Information and Propaganda, executed April 1977.
Nhim Ros, Second Vice-President of State Presidium, killed March 1978.
So Phim, First Vice-President of State Presidium, committed suicide May 1978.
Phuong, Minister of Rubber Plantations, executed June 1978.
Mey Prang, Minister of Communications, executed November 1978.

Cheng An, Minister of Industry, executed November 1978.
Vorn Vet, Deputy Premier and Minister of Economic Affairs, "committed suicide" November 1978.

The fundamental principles of what became the DK government's social and economic policy had been laid down by Khieu Samphan in his doctoral thesis submitted to the University of Paris in 1959. Samphan contended that the Cambodian economy could become independent and self-sufficient only by cutting itself off from the international economy for a time, and that only by expanding agricultural production could the base be provided for industrialization. He estimated that over 80 per cent of the urban population were unproductive and served only the élite, and advocated that they should be transferred to productive sectors of the economy, especially agriculture, and formed into co-operatives. This policy was put into effect with brutal resolution after the fall of the republican regime in April 1975.

Immediately after the capture of Phnom Penh on April 17, the city's entire population, numbering over 2,000,000, was evacuated to one of the seven zones into which Cambodia had been divided: North, North-West, East, South-East, West, North-West and Centre. Theoretically, the population of each zone fell into one of three categories: (i) "full rights" (poor peasants, lower and middle strata of the middle peasants and workers); (ii) "candidate" (upper middle peasants, wealthy peasants and petty bourgeoisie); and (iii) "depositee" (evacuees, capitalists and foreign minorities). Hence, the poorest peasants became, by dint of their impoverishment, the privileged class. As Vickery[4] has pointed out, this analysis was quite un-Marxist in that there was no recognition of the proletariat as the revolutionary vanguard, or even as a progressive class. In the provinces, the real operative division was between the evacuees (the "new" people) and those who had lived in revolutionary areas before 1975 (the "old" or "base" people).

According to official figures, about 85 per cent of the population was organized in agricultural co-operatives. As money was not in use, the co-operative members were paid in food and received one set of clothing a year. In return for surplus rice, the co-operative received a credit from the government, which was used to purchase goods which it could not produce. Conditions in the co-operatives varied considerably from place to place; in some the members were allowed to cultivate private plots of land and to keep livestock, whilst in others all property was owned communally. Conditions

[4]Michael Vickery, *Kampuchea: Politics, Economic and Society*, London 1986, pp. 29–30.

were at their most primitive in the new economic zones to which the "new" people had been sent to cultivate virgin soil, where thousands of families lived in impoverished barracks. Other "new" people, especially the young, were organized into mobile brigades up to 20,000 strong, which travelled from one site to another to build earth dams or construct artificial lakes for irrigation purposes.

Before the outbreak of war in 1970 Cambodia had been one of the most fertile food-producing areas in Indochina. Between 1970 and 1973, however, the US forces dropped over half a million tons of bombs on the food-growing areas, destroying the irrigation works and killing vast numbers of livestock. Thousands of peasants fled to the towns and cities. In consequence, a grave food crisis developed, and to feed the towns Korean rice had to be brought up the Mekong in river convoys or flown in by US aircraft.

However, after almost three years of *Khmer Rouge* rule, Pol Pot told Yugoslav journalists in March 1978 that "we have succeeded in solving the agricultural problem". His claims were to some extent supported by some foreign visitors. Others, however, suggested that the food situation remained desperately serious throughout the period of *Khmer Rouge* rule. According to refugees who escaped to Thailand and Vietnam, a poor harvest in 1975 was followed by famine conditions in the second half of 1976, and although the situation improved after good harvests in 1976 and 1977, ordinary co-operative members still received only two bowls of rice a day, while *Khmer Rouge* officials and soldiers ate meat, fish and vegetables. A large proportion of rice produced was exported or stored in the hills. In August and September 1978 the Mekong valley suffered the worst floods for 70 years, while other parts of the country faced an unprecedented drought, 10 per cent of the crop being lost.

Refugees' reports agreed that family life virtually disappeared under Pol Pot. During 1978 certain restrictions on marriage were probably relaxed as greater emphasis was placed on the need to increase the population.

Men and women were segregated and limitations were imposed on the opportunities for young people of the opposite sex to meet. Marriages had to be approved by the local co-operative authorities, and in some co-operatives husbands and wives were forced to sleep apart. According to some reports, children were taken away from their mothers when a few weeks old and entrusted to the care of people too old to labour. On the other hand, Elizabeth Becker, an American journalist who visited Cambodia in December 1978, reported that children seemed to live with their families until they were teenagers, when they were sent to factories or mobile work teams. In theory, children from the age of five onwards received elementary education in the mornings and worked in the fields for the rest of the day. In many co-operatives, however, there were reported to be either no schools at all, or at best informal classes conducted by a child or an old person who could read or write. All secondary schools and universities were closed at an early stage, but some technical schools giving training in such subjects as electrical engineering and agriculture were established.

General zonal patterns in living conditions can be inferred from refugee accounts. The South-Western and Eastern zones, the most important centres of pre-1970 communist activity, "were the best organized and most consistently administered".[5] The East, until its destruction in 1978, provided the "most favourable conditions of life, in particular for 'new' people". In contrast, the West, the North-West and most of the North-Centre were "considered 'bad' areas, where food was often short, cadres arbitrary and murderous, and policy rationales completely beyond the ken of the general populace".

Following the overthrow of the *Khmer Rouge* regime in late 1978, Pol Pot and Ieng Sary were sentenced to death in absentia by the PRK government. The indictment charged them with a long list of crimes which largely tallied with evidence earlier submitted to the UN Human Rights Commission by Western governments. According to the indictments, the *Khmer Rouge* leaders were guilty of initiating large-scale massacres, of displacing the population, establishing a system of repression and coercion, abolishing all social relationships, religion and cultural practices, ill-treating children, sabotaging the national economy and conducting terrorism.

New evidence on *Khmer Rouge* atrocities continued to come to light well after the overthrow of Pol Pot. Many mass graves containing thousands of bodies were discovered. Records at Tuol Sleng prison showed that 14,499 people had been confined there between 1975 and the end of 1978, only four of whom were known to have survived. On one single day (Oct. 15, 1977), 418 people had been executed in Tuol Sleng. In early January 1987 the PRK government released details of the "latest facts" about crimes committed by the *Khmer Rouge* regime. A figure of 3,314,718 was given for the total number of deaths attributable to the policies of the former regime. This figure was in line with the PRK's past estimates of those killed during the period, which was widely regarded as exaggerated. Official population estimates for 1984, of some 7,200,000, suggested that during the 1975–79 period the death toll (above the normal death rate) had been substantially under 1,000,000.

---

[5]Vickery, Michael, op. cit., 1984. p. 86.

WAR WITH VIETNAM

The spectacle of triumphant Communist troops marching through the streets of Phnom Penh and Saigon in April 1975 raised expectations of peace in Indochina after 30 years of foreign-instigated war. This perception ignored the fact that the victorious forces represented two countries on the verge of war, deeply divided over ideology, culture and history.

An older generation of Cambodian communists (*Khmers Viet Minh* or *Khmers Hanoi*) had close ties with their Vietnamese counterparts; they had fought alongside one another against the French, and after the 1954 Geneva accords, many had settled in North Vietnam. In Cambodia itself, this older generation of communists were replaced during the 1960s by younger Khmers who had their roots in the Paris "Marxist Circle" of the early 1950s. From 1965 onwards Viet Minh and Vietcong fighters used eastern Cambodia as a base against the South Vietnamese and US forces, with Prince Sihanouk's connivance. After two years, *Khmer Rouge* troops based in the north-east launched a guerrilla war against Sihanouk, in opposition to North Vietnam's wishes. Hanoi's appeal to the *Khmers Rouges* to defer their own revolutionary aspirations for the good of socialist internationalism bred resentment amongst Cambodian communists. It inspired not only a belief in the benefits of communist isolationism (as a preference to Vietnamese domination), but also intensified racist and ultra-nationalist tendencies within the movement.

It was such tendencies which came to the fore under *Khmer Rouge* rule, so that by mid-1978 party and government propaganda was often little more than anti-Vietnamese rhetoric. A *Black Book* published by the *Khmers Rouges* in September 1978 claimed that Cambodians never use the words "Vietnam" or Vietnamese, preferring the derogatory term "*Yuon*" instead. The "true nature" of the Vietnamese was as an "aggressor, annexationist and swallower of other countries' territories". By contrast the Pol Pot group itself held marked expansionist designs, with their endless reflections on the Angkor epoch and their promises to "liberate" the ethnic Khmers of *Kampuchea Krom* (Vietnam's Mekong delta region) and the Thai provinces of Surin and Buriram.

It was against such a background of racist resentment that a large group of *Khmer Hanoi* returned to Cambodia after Sihanouk's overthrow in 1970. They were gradually liquidated, and at the same time Vietnamese troops operating in Cambodia were treated with great suspicion by *Khmer Rouge* forces which occasionally mounted attacks against them.

Border clashes began immediately after the fall of Phnom Penh and Saigon in April 1975. This small-scale fighting, which was instigated almost entirely by Cambodia, stopped prior to a visit by Pol Pot to Hanoi in mid-June. The situation remained generally peaceful for the rest of 1975 and the whole of 1976. However, periods of intense internal opposition to Pol Pot during 1975–76 were subsequently characterized by the *Khmer Rouge* government as Vietnamese-instigated *coup* attempts.

In January 1977, Cambodian forces from the South-Western zone (i.e. those under the command of Ta Mok) launched large-scale attacks on villages and Army posts in six of Vietnam's western border provinces. At the same time tension mounted on Cambodia's frontier with Thailand and, to a lesser extent, Laos. The ferocity of the Cambodian attacks increased in April and May and in mid-year the fighting, which had previously been confined mainly to the area between the Mekong and the coast, spread to the Parrot's Beak area and even to the Central Highlands of Vietnam.

The scale of the fighting again increased in the second half of September 1977, the period of Pol Pot's public emergence as the general secretary of the Cambodian Communist Party and of his visit to Beijing [see above]. According to Vietnamese reports (supported by US intelligence assessments) Cambodian forces totalling about four divisions launched continuous attacks from Sept. 24 onwards along the entire border of Nay Ninh province. Over 1,000 civilians were killed or wounded in this area between September and November. The *Khmers Rouges*, on the other hand, alleged that Cambodia was invaded in September by several Vietnamese divisions, supported by hundreds of tanks, artillery and aircraft.

Finally, in mid-December, Vietnam reacted to the *Khmer Rouge* provocation and launched a counter-offensive into Cambodia. Vietnam kept her troops in Cambodia for only a matter of weeks before attempting to organize peace negotiations, the first of a series of Vietnamese initiatives that were consistently rejected out of hand by Pol Pot.

The *Khmer Rouge* government responded to the offensive by breaking diplomatic relations with Vietnam in late December. The next month they launched a propaganda offensive, claiming that the retreating Vietnamese forces had been "routed shamefully". A Cambodian broadcast on Jan. 6, 1978, claimed that over 29,000 Vietnamese troops had been killed or wounded for the loss of only 470 Cambodians. *Le Monde* described these claims as "completely incredible", a view shared by most commentators.

During the first months of 1978, the Vietnamese forces remained largely on the defensive, repelling repeated Cambodian raids across the border. It was during this period that the final remnants of the relatively pro-Vietnamese internal opposition in Cambodia were brutally extinguished in the Eastern zone massacres [see above]. From this point onwards, any hopes harboured by Hanoi that the aggressively chauvinist nature of the Cambodian revolution might be altered internally were dispelled. At the same time, relations between Vietnam and China deteriorated sharply. Thousands of the Chinese (Hoa) community in Vietnam left for China, and, in July, Chinese economic aid to Vietnam was finally cut off. The Soviet Union reponded by adopting a strongly pro-Vietnamese attitude, repeatedly accusing China of responsibility for the conflict.

VIETNAM'S INVASION AND THE OVERTHROW OF POL POT

Following the death of So Phim and the start of the Eastern Zone massacres in May 1978, Hanoi began to organize an anti-Pol Pot resistance movement among Cambodian refugees. These were situated in western Vietnam and in areas of the Eastern Zone "liberated" by Vietnamese forces in mid-1978 in support of So Phim's rebellion. By the end of October 1978 Vietnam had some 100,000 troops stationed along the Cambodian border, under the command of Gen. Hoang Cham. The Cambodian anti-Pol Pot forces, operating mainly as small guerrilla units, numbered somewhere between 10,000 and 20,000. The *Khmer Rouge* troops along the border numbered about 60,000.

On Dec. 3 some 200 of the leading survivors of Pol Pot's crackdown on the Eastern Zone met in a "liberated" area of that zone to form the "Cambodian National United Front for National Salvation (CNUFNS). Led by Heng Samrin, So Phim's deputy military commander, the CNUFNS central committee also included Chea Sim, Mat Ly, Hun Sen, Mean Saman, Meas Samnang, Neou Samon, Chan Ven, Hem Samin and Prach Sun.

On Dec. 25, some 100,000 Vietnamese and 20,000 CNUFNS troops, under the direction of Gen. Van Tien Dung, the Vietnamese Army Chief of Staff and the officer in charge of the final communist offensive in South Vietnam in 1975, advanced into Cambodia in several directions simultaneously. Proceeding so rapidly that they had no time to occupy the territory they had overrun, the invading forces had virtually encircled Phnom Penh by Jan. 6, 1979. A broadcast by the CNUFNS the next day suggested that only two of Cambodia's 19 provinces—Oddor Meanchey in the north-west and Pursat in the west—were still in the hands of Pol Pot's forces. Phnom Penh had apparently been entered unopposed, the city having been evacuated by the Pol Pot government and the garrison.

The establishment of a "People's Revolutionary Council" (PRC), headed by Heng Samrin, to act as a provisional government was announced in Phnom Penh on Jan. 8. The PRC declared on Jan. 10 that the "dictatorial, fascist and genocidal regime of the reactionary Pol Pot–Ieng Sary clique" had been completely abolished and the People's Republic of Kampuchea (PRK) established in its place.

The new government was recognized by Vietnam and Laos and by the Soviet Union and its allies. The West responded by roundly criticizing the Vietnamese invasion; many countries announced the suspension of aid to Hanoi. On Jan. 15, a resolution calling for the withdrawal of all foreign forces from Cambodia was adopted by the council by 13 votes to two, but was vetoed by the Soviet Union. Over the years, as the extent of *Khmer Rouge* atrocities has become clearer, many independent observers have come to agree with Vickery[6] in his description of the Vietnamese invasion as a "legitimate act of self-defence undertaken in support of one faction of the previous Cambodian regime, just as the latter, when they were in revolutionary opposition, had accepted Vietnamese and Chinese aid in their war against Lon Nol's Khmer Republic, and in the same way that Lon Nol had required American, Thai and (Republican) Vietnamese aid to maintain himself after overthrowing the legally constituted government of Prince Sihanouk. With respect to the reliance on foreign support for survival and the acquisition of state power by force, the status of the PRK is no more invidious than that of its two most recent predecessors. Since Lon Nol's Khmer Republic was rapidly granted international recognition, and since Pol Pot's Democratic Kampuchea was also recognized by most of the world and given Cambodia's seat in the United Nations, there would seem to be few valid reasons for withholding similar recognition from the PRK".

[6]Vickery, Michael, 1986. op. cit. p 42.

FAMINE AND DIVISION

THE THREAT OF FAMINE—THE POLITICS OF AID

A major food crisis, which in some areas reached famine proportions, developed in Cambodia during the chaotic months following Pol Pot's overthrow. The country's potentially rich agricultural system had been badly damaged during the carnage of 1970–75 and further destruction had been caused by the wholesale transfer of population carried out by the Pol Pot regime. Large areas of land adjacent to Vietnam in south-eastern Cambodia had been taken out of cultivation by the *Khmers Rouges* to prevent contact between Khmer and Vietnamese peasants. Drought and floods ruined the crops in 1978, and after Vietnam's military intervention the retreating *Khmers Rouges* carried off all the food they could, destroyed the remaining stocks, together with the rice ready to be harvested, and killed livestock. Millions of people who had been forcibly moved to distant provinces by the *Khmers Rouges* abandoned agricultural work to return to their former homes or to search for their lost families. Most people, freed after months of enforced malnutrition, ate whatever was available, including vital rice seed and work animals.

By February 1979 the new government warned that "the quantity of rice currently available to the people is negligible". Officials of the International Red Cross and UNICEF who visited Phnom Penh at the government's invitation in July estimated that over two million people were facing starvation. The scale of the impending catastrophe in Cambodia was only fully revealed to the West in September 1979 with the showing of a television documentary by journalist John Pilger, detailing the grave situation in the country. Up until early October, Western food aid to Cambodia had totalled a meagre 200 tonnes. Only Vietnam and the Soviet Union had responded immediately to the PRK government's appeals for food aid, and by early November both had delivered a total of 280,000 tonnes.

The West's, and in particular America's, reticent attitude towards the provision of emergency aid to Phnom Penh stemmed from its reluctance to provide a measure of legitimacy to Vietnam's "occupation" of Cambodia. Hence, during early 1979 the Carter administration opposed the provision of any aid to the PRK and dismissed the rumours of approaching famine as alarmist. As the severity of the situation became irrefutable, the USA, wary of blemishing its humanitarian image, dropped its opposition to an international aid effort. However, it stressed that it would only approve the "neutral" distribution of aid (i.e. disbursement to the PRK government and to the anti-PRK forces—principally the *Khmers Rouges*—massing on Thailand's borders). The "neutrality" proviso provoked strong condemnation from Phnom Penh, but, ultimately, the government was in no position to make demands of the West. In late September the PRK granted approval to the Red Cross and UNICEF for large-scale relief operations in Cambodia, even though both organizations were also distributing aid in the *Khmers Rouges*-controlled Thai border area. Nevertheless, the USA continued its campaign of vilification against the PRK regime throughout 1979, alleging, amongst other things, that Vietnam was stealing aid intended for the starving in Cambodia.

At a UN conference in New York in early November, 51 countries pledged aid worth US$210 million in cash and kind, with the largest contributions coming from the USA ($29,000,000) and the European Community ($42,000,000). The aid was to go to famine relief inside Cambodia, and also to refugees in Thai camps and on the Thai border. After the conference, Western aid began to flow into Cambodia in increasing quantities. The distribution of food was hampered by inadequate transport facilities, however; only one locomotive was working properly on the railway from the main port at Kompong Som to Phnom Penh and there was a shortage of lorries. A UNICEF spokesman said in early December that food was reaching most of the 70,000 people in the capital, but less than 10 per cent of that intended for the rural areas was arriving. The bulk of the aid was stockpiled in warehouses, and as these filled up towards the end of the year, international deliveries were reduced.

Once distribution improved, the government prioritized the delivery of seed rice to "production solidarity groups" (*krom samaki*) which it had encouraged people to form. These groups usually consisted of between 10 to 15 families working on either their own or communal rice land, pooling labour, tools and animals. Production incentives were increased by the government's initial reliance on *laissez-faire*, with no taxes on agricultural products and no obligatory contribution to the state. To further encourage the "family economy" (in other words, private enterprise), and to promote the expansion of agricultural production, a decree published in March 1980 provided for the re-introduction of money into the Cambodian economy. Money had been abolished by the *Khmer Rouge* regime, with wages being paid in food rations. After the establishment of the PRK, trade had been conducted with rice, gold and Vietnamese and Thai money.

The food situation improved at the beginning of 1980. With the aid of Soviet experts, the handling of food shipments at Kompong Som was accelerated and storage capacity at the port increased from 25,000 to 90,000 tonnes, whilst the supply of Soviet lorries speeded up distribution. Most people had returned to their homes and the winter harvest had been safely reaped. It had not been a good one, however; only about 30 per cent of the agricultural land had been planted, and in some areas the crop was lost through floods or drought. Faced with the continuing shortfall, the government adopted a policy of leaving locally produced rice in the countryside and using imported food to meet the needs of the urban population.

The situation at the start of 1981 was summed up in a report published by the UN Food and Agriculture Organization (FAO) which warned that while starvation in Cambodia had been overcome, the economy remained in a very fragile condition. The report concluded that without further international assistance serious malnutrition could quickly return. Production in 1980 had been considerably higher than in the previous year, but the yield was not sufficient to feed the entire population adequately. The food situation deteriorated during 1981, largely as a result of bad weather conditions. Flooding in the south-eastern provinces and drought in the west and south-west meant that Cambodia remained dependent on relief aid during the 1982 rainy season. Nevertheless, visitors to the country brought back optimistic reports that contrasted sharply with the doom-laden predictions of large sections of the Bangkok-based Western media. In 1982 an improvement in the weather took place, and the harvest left a rice deficit of only 207,000 tonnes, compared with 446,000 tonnes the previous year.

As the threat of famine diminished, the political aspect of the West's aid operation in Cambodia became increasingly prominent. Western donors, led by the USA, had been pressing the UN for some time to implement a complete halt to operations inside Cambodia, and to channel all aid through the refugee camps along the Thai border. By 1982 such a policy was effectively in operation, so that aid became little more than a political instrument to bolster the anti-PRK forces. The United Nations maintained that distribution was strictly supervised in order to prevent aid being given directly to armed groups, but as actual distribution was usually carried out by the Thai military, this was difficult to verify. Vietnam and the Soviet Union maintained their embargo on participation with the UN, preferring to channel their aid directly through Phnom Penh.

Western aid donors and the UN agencies which operated in Cambodia during the emergency years (1979–82) were subsequently barred from supplying Phnom Penh with "development aid" of any sort. This arose because the majority of UN General Assembly members continued to recognize the *Khmer Rouge* government after 1979 in protest at Vietnam's "occupation" of Cambodia. As a consequence, the UN and donor countries were encouraged to respond with emergency assistance to food shortages in Cambodia, but were obstructed in their efforts to provide the necessary equipment and training to prevent such shortages in the first place. With little long-term development, Cambodia has continued to be dependent on emergency supplies of aid to its poor agricultural areas.

THE REFUGEE PROBLEM

Cambodia's refugee problem has its origins in the carnage of the 1970–75 War, when approximately half of the country's population were uprooted. The majority of those displaced by the war remained within Cambodia's borders, leaving villages and entering cities. Some middle class Cambodians fled to Thailand and large numbers of ethnic Vietnamese escaped to South Vietnam in order to escape Lon Nol's pogroms.

Approximately 60,000 Cambodians fled to Vietnam during the first year of *Khmer Rouge* rule, whilst just over 20,000 had entered Thailand by late 1976. The flow decreased during 1977, partly as a result of the establishment of stricter security precautions on both sides of the Thai-Cambodian border, but picked up again the following year, as refugees flooded into both Thailand and Vietnam to escape renewed purges within Cambodia. For the first time, the refugees included a number of *Khmer Rouge* officials and soldiers. Their escape was assisted by a relaxation of security precautions on the Thai border caused by the transfer of troops to the Vietnamese frontier.

Only a small number of Khmers crossed the border into Thailand during the immediate aftermath of the Vietnamese invasion of Cambodia in late 1978; of these, the majority appeared to be middle-class survivors of the Pol Pot years, desperate to escape the country at all cost. The massive flow of Khmers into Thailand began in April 1979, when Vietnamese forces launched attacks on *Khmer Rouge* units accumulating on the Thai-Cambodian border. Those crossing into Thailand were a mixture of genuine civilian refugees escaping the heavy fighting and *Khmer Rouge* soldiers sheltering from the Vietnamese onslaught. As the fighting subsided in late June, there were at least 250,000 Cambodians encamped along the border.

The Kriangsak government in Thailand, anxious to avoid being encumbered with millions of starving Khmers, refused to grant the Cambodians refugee status. Instead, they were deemed "illegal entrants" and the United Nations High Commissioner for Refugees (UNHCR) was denied access to them. The first forced repatriations took place in early June 1979, when almost 43,000 Cambodians were transferred from the border town of Aranyaprathet to the frontier of the northern Cambodian province of Preah Vihear. Many of those expelled by the Thai Army subsequently died, either blown up by landmines or executed by *Khmer Rouge* soldiers. International pressure forced the Thai government to alter its policy, and in late June a decision to repatriate a further 42,000 Cambodians was reversed.

Increasing numbers of Cambodians, many of them suffering from serious malnutrition, entered Thailand during the second half of 1979. By the end of the year there were as many as 1,000,000 in various camps along the border. In October, Vietnamese forces launched another fierce attack against the *Khmers Rouges*, again driving large numbers of Pol Pot's cadres into Thailand, where they regrouped at Sakaeo. The refugee situation was transformed in mid-October when Gen. Kriangsak announced that there would be "no more forced repatriation" of Cambodians. By advocating an "open door" policy, the Thai government ensured that the major international aid effort for Cambodia would be directed not towards Phnom Penh, but along the border. The Thais made an official request for UN emergency assistance on Nov. 1 and within three weeks a UNHCR refugee transit centre was opened at Khao I Dang, some 12 km from Aranyaprathet.

Those entering Khao I Dang were granted *de facto* refugee status, making them eligible for resettlement in third countries. However, the majority (regarded as "displaced persons" and not refugees) remained in makeshift camps along the border. These camps, populated by both civilians and guerrilla fighters (*Khmers Rouges* and non-communist *Khmers Serei*), were at the centre of a massive, illegal cross-border trading system. Heavy with UN food and medicine, they acted as rear-base camps for the guerrillas, the civilian portion serving as a buffer against Vietnamese attack. Eventually the border camps came under the administration of the three component members of the exile tripartite Coalition Government of Democratic Kampuchea [CGDK—see below].

The military nature of the camps was demonstrated clearly in the first half of 1980, when Thailand initiated a policy of "voluntary repatriation". This amounted to little more than a bolstering of the *Khmer Rouge* ranks ahead of their wet season offensive. Vietnam responded by launching surprise attacks in late June on *Khmer Serei* camps on the Thai frontier in the area north-east of Aranyaprathet and Poipet.

Between 1980 and 1984 a pattern emerged, with Vietnamese and PRK forces carrying out dry season offensives against guerrilla positions on the border. Civilians in the camps (theoretically situated on Cambodian soil) would move into eastern Thailand for the duration of the fighting before returning to Cambodian camps for the wet season. Vietnamese successes during the 1984–85 offensive [see below] prompted the creation of new evacuation sites for "displaced" Cambodians in Thailand. Built with the aid of the UN and various NGOs, the eight new camps were patrolled by the specially-created Thai Task Force 80 and were under the control of CGDK leaders.

The *Khmers Rouges* currently administer five camps (Natrao, Huay Chan, Ta Luan, Bo Rai and Site 8) with a combined population of approximately 60,000. The Sihanoukists and the KPNLF run one camp each, Site B and Site 2 respectively, the first with a population in excess of 40,000, and the second providing accommodation for over 160,000 Khmers. Khao I Dang, where some 15,000 Cambodian "refugees" await resettlement, was officially closed down at the beginning of 1987. Its inhabitants were to be placed under the control of the non-communist elements of the CGDK. However, although the camp remains officially closed, refugees were still there in mid-1989.

GUERRILLA RESISTANCE

Vietnam's 1978 incursion into neighbouring Cambodia was accomplished with rehearsed precision by well armed, battled-hardened troops. As many as 30,000 *Khmer Rouge* soldiers were killed or injured in the fighting and the remainder were left with little choice but to retreat into the swamps and mountains of the Cambodian countryside. By early 1979 some 15,000 *Khmer Rouge* remnants had found their way to the western provinces of Battambang, Pursat and Koh Kong, in the area between Highway 5 and the Cardamom mountains; an equal number were scattered over the rest of the country in small guerrilla bands.

In March and April 1979, the Vietnamese launched a series of attacks designed to clear the *Khmers Rouges* from the western lands. On the whole, the operation was successful, forcing the guerrillas to retreat, more often than not into the relative safety of eastern Thailand. By mid-1979, as the rainy season set in, the Vietnamese forces controlled all but the outlying Western districts of Cambodia. By containing the *Khmers Rouges* in these largely uninhabited districts, Vietnam effectively denied them the opportunity to recruit the fresh fighters necessary to conduct a successful guerrilla war.

Faced with the prospect of annihilation by the Vietnamese Army, the *Khmers Rouges* concentrated their efforts on pursuing their international rehabilitation. The Chinese government, bound by regional imperatives, continued to support them; arms shipments via Thailand started in February 1979. In the same month Deng Xiaoping ordered large numbers of Chinese troops into northern Vietnam in an attempt to "punish" Hanoi for its invasion of Cambodia. Other countries were less inclined to tender their immediate support to the *Khmers Rouges*, who were, by late 1979, widely reviled on account of their genocidal practices of the previous three years. In a blatant attempt to redress this impression, the *Khmers Rouges* released details of a new "liberal" political programme in September 1979. This appeared to pay dividends, when, following a lengthy debate on the representation of Cambodia, the UN General Assembly decided in mid-September that the country should continue to be represented at the UN by the "Democratic Kampuchea" regime (i.e. the *Khmer Rouge* government). In a further attempt to improve its image, Khieu Samphan was appointed as the *Khmer Rouge* Prime Minister in December; Pol Pot, the outgoing Premier, was appointed C.-in-C. of the armed forces.

In addition to the *Khmers Rouges*, the Thai-Cambodian border was also a refuge for some 6,000 *Khmers Serei* fighters. The term *Khmers Serei* was originally applied to right-wing guerrillas who operated on the Thai frontier in the 1960s, supported the Lon Nol regime in the early 1970s and resumed their guerrilla activities after the establishment of the Pol Pot regime in 1975. During 1979–80, the *Khmers Serei* were a disparate cluster of warring factions. By 1981, however, an element of order had been restored to their ranks. They were divided into two factions; those loyal to former Prime Minister Son Sann, grouped together as the Khmer People's National Liberation Front (KPNLF); and those loyal to Prince Sihanouk, termed, variously, *Moulinaka* or *Armée Nationale Sihanoukiste* (ANS). The *Khmers Rouges*, the KPNLF and the Sihanoukists generally observed an informal truce, the former being concentrated south and the latter north of Highway 5, but clashes between them sometimes occurred as a result of disagreements over international relief supplies and recruiting in refugee camps.

Fighting between Vietnamese forces and the rebels, mainly the *Khmers Rouges*, continued during early 1981, and on a reduced scale after the onset of the rainy season in May. From February onwards, the *Khmers Rouges* generally took the initiative, with the aim of disrupting elections due to be held in the PRK [see below]. After the dry season began in October,

Vietnamese troops, supported by an increased PRK military contingent, launched their biggest offensive since 1979. For the first time in the war, the Vietnamese made regular use of aircraft for bombing and troop carrying. In December 1981 the *Khmers Rouges* suffered a devastating setback when Son Sen (their Defence Minister) was forced to evacuate his jungle base in northern Cambodia. The offensive continued during the early months of 1982 and was described by commentators as the most intense and sustained campaign since 1979. Nevertheless, guerrilla activities inside Cambodia continued during the wet season from May onwards, with the majority of recorded incidents being ascribed to the *Khmers Rouges*.

Faced with defeat on the battlefield, and under increasing pressure from sympathetic ASEAN states to present a united front, the three Cambodian rebel factions eventually agreed to form a single "Coalition Government of Democratic Kampuchea" (CGDK), in June 1982, with Sihanouk as its head [see following chapter]. In practice, however, this new-found unity did little to improve the rebels' military position. Two years of relative military stalemate followed until late 1984, when the Vietnamese–PRK forces launched their heaviest attacks of the war. The 1984–1985 dry season was marked by a series of victories over the rebel armies. By March 1985 all of the main CGDK bases along the Thai frontier had been overrun, including *Khmer Rouge* strongholds in the mountains of Phnom Malai, the KPNLF headquarters at Ampil and the Sihanoukist base at Tatum. Having dislodged the CGDK guerrilla bases from the border area, Vietnamese and PRK forces started to implement the so-called "K–5" plan aimed at stabilizing the security situation in Cambodia. This involved mining and clearing the jungle at border crossing points and carrying out improvements on the roads and supply lines.

Over the next four years the Vietnamese–PRK forces continued to consolidate their position on the border, laying large numbers of mines and constructing a large, spiked fence. The rebel forces, and particularly the *Khmers Rouges*, had established a number of small units within Cambodia following the destruction of the CGDK bases during the 1984–85 dry season. Vietnamese and PRK forces adopted an essentially reactive role, responding to CGDK activity rather than launching their own attacks.

The *Khmers Rouges* claimed to have carried out numerous sustained attacks upon Vietnamese forces during the 1985–89 period. According to these reports, which were almost never independently confirmed and were widely regarded as exaggerated, the *Khmers Rouges* were operating freely in the western border areas and in the interior, including Phnom Penh and the *Tonle Sap*. Some press reports claimed that the *Khmers Rouges* were storing weapons in "friendly" villages in preparation for the eventual withdrawal of Vietnamese troops. The

leaders that the proposals represented a significant change in Vietnam's strategy towards Cambodia.

DIPLOMATIC STALEMATE, 1982–87

The diplomatic pattern of proposal and counter-proposal, established during the early 1980s continued during 1983–85, with neither the Indochinese or ASEAN camps making any significant concessions. The principle barrier halting the opening of negotiations appeared to be the reluctance of the ASEAN/CGDK side to accept Vietnam's proposition that the conflict was an internal Cambodian affair, to be settled by the opposing Khmer factions. They maintained that Vietnam's "occupation" of Cambodia was the crux of the matter, and that any negotiations had therefore to centre on Hanoi and not Phnom Penh.

Vietnam claimed to have withdrawn a number of military units from Cambodia during 1982–85, but such withdrawals were dismissed by China and ASEAN as routine troop rotations. In August 1985, however, the Indochinese governments announced that all Vietnamese troops in Cambodia (officially termed as "volunteer forces"), would be withdrawn by the end of 1990.

The rebel factions continued to be plagued with division, and there were reports of fighting between the component armies. During late 1985 and early 1986, the KPNLF, in particular, suffered from serious divisions within the leadership. Nevertheless, "non lethal" aid of up to $5,000,000 for the non-communist components of the CGDK (i.e. the KPNLF and the Sihanoukists but not the *Khmers Rouges*) was incorporated in the US Foreign Aid Bill signed by President Reagan in August 1985.

In March 1986, the CGDK issued its so-called "eight-point proposal", which was subsequently adopted as its national charter. The proposal called for the withdrawal of Vietnamese forces from Cambodia and the possible formation of a quadripartite government comprising PRK and CGDK officials. The proposal was rejected by the PRK, who claimed that it was designed to cover up the rebels' military losses. In January 1987 the PRK formally offered to meet CGDK representatives (excluding Pol Pot and Ieng Sary) for discussions. The offer was rejected, although Sihanouk was thought to have welcomed the initiative. A few months later, Hanoi and Phnom Penh both accepted an Indonesian proposal to attend informal "cocktail party" talks in Jakarta in July. However, they later rejected revisions made to the original Indonesian proposal by the other ASEAN countries which called for a more substantial level of Vietnamese involvement in the proposed talks.

In a significant break with past policy Hun Sen declared in late September that the *Khmers Rouges* might have "a role to play in the solution" to the Cambodian conflict and that he was prepared to meet with Khieu Samphan. The PRK issued a five-point peace proposal in October, which included offers on PRK–CGDK talks, Vietnam's troop withdrawal, internationally-supervised elections and an international conference.

THE FIRST HUN SEN–SIHANOUK MEETING

The first substantive negotiations between the opposing Cambodian factions were held in France in December 1987 and January 1988. Hun Sen and Sihanouk met, first, in early December, at the Prince's residence in Fère-en-Tardenois and then again, in mid-January, at Saint Germain-en-Laye. Son Sann and Khieu Samphan had both refused to attend the talks unless a Vietnamese delegation was also present.

Hun Sen told reporters after the second round of talks that he and Sihanouk were in broad agreement on the question of the political structure of a post-settlement Cambodia. Both had agreed that a coalition government (to include members of the three CGDK groups and PRK officials) should be formed. However, they had disagreed over the timing of the establishment of such a government in relation to the holding of a general election; Hun Sen favoured elections followed by the formation of a government, Sihanouk the reverse. The two also disagreed on the timetable for Vietnamese troops withdrawal.

In an effort to break the deadlock, the Vietnamese Defence Ministry announced details of a plan to withdraw 50,000 "Army volunteers" from Cambodia during 1988. The announcement was thought to be linked to the Reagan–Gorbachev summit meeting in Moscow taking place at the same time. Under the plan, 50,000 Vietnamese troops would be pulled out between June and December 1988. The remaining Vietnamese forces (estimated at some 70,000) would be placed under the control of PRK commanders before being withdrawn entirely by 1990. Phnom Penh radio also announced that the remaining Vietnamese troops would be pulled back at least 30 kilometres from the Thai-Cambodian border.

Although the withdrawal took place as planned the *Khmers Rouges* and the Chinese government accused Vietnam of "befuddling world opinion" by disguising tens of thousands of its troops as PRK soldiers. Despite such claims, there was a measure of international anxiety that the withdrawal would allow the *Khmers Rouges* to regain the military ascendancy in Cambodia. Although the

PRK's own 35,000-strong Army had been well trained by Vietnamese advisers, it was widely believed that the *Khmers Rouges* were a superior fighting force. In an attempt to redress the balance of power within the CGDK and to curb the influence of the *Khmers Rouges*, the USA decided in September 1988 to treble its aid to the two non-communist factions.

FACE TO FACE AT JIM 1

The first face-to-face talks between the four Cambodian factions eventually took place in Indonesia in July 1988, under the guise of the "Jakarta Informal Meeting" known as "JIM 1". Two weeks before the meeting Sihanouk had resigned the CGDK presidency in an attempt to "weaken and isolate the *Khmers Rouges*". The mercurial Prince had resumed the presidency in late February 1988, after announcing his "irreversible" resignation in January.

Sihanouk attended the four-day meeting in a private capacity, foregoing the formal sessions. Also in attendance were Hun Sen, Son Sann, Khieu Samphan and representatives of the governments of Vietnam, Laos and the six ASEAN countries.

The CGDK, with the support of the ASEAN contingent, presented a proposal to the meeting which, among other things, posited a three-stage process of Vietnamese troop withdrawal. During the second stage, the Phnom Penh government would be dismantled and replaced by a provisional four-party coalition headed by Sihanouk, with elections following in the third stage. The second stage was rejected by the PRK, who proposed instead the creation of a Sihanouk-headed national reconciliation council representing all the factions. The PRK also linked the withdrawal of the Vietnamese "volunteer forces" to the immediate cessation of Chinese assistance to the *Khmers Rouges*.

POST-JIM NEGOTIATIONS

Following the apparent stalemate at the JIM, hopes for a settlement centred on talks which convened in August 1988 between the Soviet Union and China. Deputy Foreign Ministers Igor Rogachev and Tian Zengpei met for four days in Beijing, but despite some evidence of progress, no breakthrough was achieved. The main source of friction was China's continued backing of the *Khmers Rouges*. Beijing saw its support for the *Khmers Rouges* as being intrinsically linked with the military threat which it perceived from Vietnam. During the course of the year, however, indications suggested

China was considering moderating its position with regard to the *Khmers Rouges*. For example, in mid-November, the Chinese Premier, Li Peng, affirmed that China would never support the *Khmers Rouges*'s return to exclusive power.

In early November 1988 the UN General Assembly adopted a resolution sponsored by the six ASEAN states calling for the withdrawal of "all foreign forces" from Cambodia. In itself, this was not significant; similar resolutions had been passed each year for the past 10 years. The 1988 resolution, however contained a number of important revisions over previous years. It included provisions for the guaranteed withdrawal of foreign forces "under the supervision and control of an international commission". The resolution also called for "the creation of an interim administrating authority" to rule the country in the period between a troop withdrawal and the holding of elections. It went on to urge "the promotion of national reconciliation among all Cambodians" under Sihanouk.

Most strikingly, the new resolution contained a clear warning to the *Khmers Rouges*, affirming that there could be "no return to universally condemned policies and practices of a recent past" in Cambodia. It dropped all reference to the International Conference on Cambodia, which had been established by the UN in 1980 as a forum for peace negotiations. In its place, it offered support to "any other conference of an international nature under the auspices of the [UN] Secretary-General".

THE PACE QUICKENS

Efforts to negotiate an end to the conflict accelerated in January 1989, with Vietnam proposing a speeding-up of its troop withdrawal timetable, and talks taking place between the chief regional protagonists.

The most significant meeting was between Hun Sen and the Thai Prime Minister, Chatichai Choonhaven, in late January. Thai officials stressed that this was "informal" and did not imply any recognition of the PRK regime. Chatichai claimed that he merely wished to play a "facilitating role" between the warring factions. Sihanouk, however, expressed anger at Hun Sen's visit, saying that the invitation would confuse international opinion. Also in January, Vietnam and China had their first direct contact since 1979, with a visit to Beijing by Deputy Foreign Minister Dinh Nho Liem.

All this increased diplomatic activity was in part a consequence of improved relations between China and the Soviet Union, both of whom had acknowledged the conflict as one of the "three obstacles" to the further normalization of bilateral relations. This was reflected in a nine-point Sino-Soviet statement on Cambodia which was formulated during a visit to China by Soviet Foreign Minister Shevardnadze in February. According to the statement, agreement had been reached on: (i) the need for an "effective control mechanism" to supervise the Vietnamese troop withdrawal; (ii) an end to foreign military aid to the warring factions; (iii) the holding of national elections; (iv) an "appropriate role" for the UN; and (v) the convening of an international conference. Disagreement remained over the nature of the transitional government to be set up in Cambodia following the Vietnamese withdrawal.

Expectations of further progress were high during the run-up to Mikhail Gorbachev's visit to China in May 1989. In the event, however, this was completely overshadowed by massive pro-democracy student demonstrations which coincided with his time in Beijing. Gorbachev discussed Cambodia with China's leader, Deng Xiaoping, but no breakthrough was reported and both sides reaffirmed their commitment to the February nine-point statement.

STALEMATE AT JIM 2

The second Indonesian-sponsored meeting of the various Cambodian factions and other "interested parties" (JIM 2) was held in Jakarta in mid-February 1989. A matter of days before the meeting started, Sihanouk announced that he had resumed the CGDK presidency; he claimed that he had a duty, as a patriot, to "retake the helm". However, Sihanouk's displeasure over Chatichai Choonhaven's January meeting with Hun Sen was believed to lie behind his subsequent decision not to attend JIM 2, where he was represented by his son Prince Norodom Ranaridh.

Ali Alatas, the JIM 2 chair, introduced a working paper at preparatory talks which attempted to strike a compromise between the opposing factions on the elections question. The Alatas proposal allowed for both the Hun Sen government and the CGDK to continue to function while elections were being held for a new Cambodian Assembly. He also presented a series of options for an international control mechanism to supervise the Vietnamese withdrawal, the ceasefire and elections. However, opposing Cambodian officials refused to make the concessions needed to forge any meaningful agreement. As the talks progressed to full ministerial level, it appeared that the rival factions had actually hardened their respective positions on the two most intractable issues: the formation of a provisional quadripartite government and the composition and size of the proposed "control mechanism". Despite the lack of real progress at the talks, a "consensus statement" was issued at the close which allowed for further negotiations towards a comprehensive settlement.

TROOP WITHDRAWAL BREAKTHROUGH

In a dramatic turnabout the three Indochinese governments issued a joint statement on April 5 announcing that all Vietnamese "volunteer troops" would be withdrawn from Cambodia by the end of September 1989, regardless of whether or not a political solution to the conflict had been found. Vietnam had previously stipulated that its troops would return home in September only if foreign military aid to the CGDK was halted.

The joint statement called for the cessation of foreign interference in Cambodia's internal affairs and for the ending of all foreign military aid to the various factions by the end of September. It warned that if foreign countries (a reference primarily to China) continued to arm Cambodian rebels after the September deadline, then the PRK reserved "its legitimate right to call on other countries to give [military] assistance". The statement also proposed that the International Control and Supervision Commission for the Implementation of the 1954 Geneva agreements (comprising India, Poland and Canada) be reactivated to monitor the Vietnamese withdrawal and to ensure a simultaneous cut-off of foreign military supplies to the CGDK forces.

The six ASEAN countries, along with the USA and other Western nations, responded to the statement with cautious optimism. Sihanouk, however, was dismissive, declaring that he "diametrically rejected all decisions, conditions and agreements on Cambodia made by Vietnam, Laos and the foreign lackey Phnom Penh regime".

Diplomatic activity intensified during the weeks leading up to the mid-May Sino-Soviet summit [see above]. At the end of April, the Phnom Penh regime announced a series of constitutional amendments intended as concessions in the lead-up to talks at the beginning of May between Hun Sen, Son Sann and Sihanouk in Jakarta. The PRK was renamed the State of Cambodia and the country's national flag, national anthem and national coat of arms were altered. Buddhism was elevated to the national religion and the death penalty was abolished.

At a press conference given after his talks with Sihanouk, Hun Sen said that agreement had been reached on the cessation of arms supplies to all parties after Vietnam's troop withdrawal. He announced his intention to invite Sihanouk to return to Cambodia as head of state and later proposed the establishment of a supreme council comprising members of his government alongside CGDK representatives. The council would be based in Phnom Penh, and its main task would be to prepare for elections in November. Sihanouk rejected Hun Sen's "supreme council" formula, proposing instead the establishment of a four-faction government to prepare for elections. However, he confirmed that he had dropped his earlier demand for an outright dismantling of the Phnom Penh administration, and declared his willingness to return to Phnom Penh in late 1989 on condition that Vietnam's troop withdrawal had been internationally verified, that a multi-party system had been enshrined in the constitution and that a ceasefire was in force.

The question of a ceasefire figured prominently in talks between Hun Sen and Chatichai Choonhaven in Bangkok on May 5. After the talks, the Thai Prime Minister called on all the Cambodian combatants to lay down their arms. Chatichai's plea was rejected by Khieu Samphan, who denounced Vietnam's withdrawal plan as a mere manoeuvre designed to cling to power and called for the dismantling of the Phnom Penh regime.

Samphan's hardline remarks notwithstanding, the *Khmers Rouges* were coming under increasing pressure from China and their CGDK partners to cultivate a more humane image ahead of an international conference on Cambodia planned for late July.

In early June, Pol Pot was reported to have resigned from his last official *Khmer Rouge* post, that of director for the Higher Institute for National Defence. At the same time, Chhit Choeun (Ta Mok), announced that he would "cease all activities within Cambodian state [i.e. CGDK] organizations" when Vietnamese troops had withdrawn. Mok was one of the most powerful *Khmer Rouge* officers, commanding the loyalty of some 10,000 men.

As Cambodia's leader for most of the 45-month period of *Khmer Rouge* rule, Pol Pot had come to symbolize the regime's brutal and arrogant single-mindedness, and his continued presence within the CGDK administration constituted an increasingly serious obstacle to a settlement of the conflict. Commentators reacted to the announcement with some scepticism, believing that Pol Pot would continue to exercise considerable military influence. His previous "resignation" as Chairman of the *Khmer Rouge* Supreme Military Commission in September 1985 had also been greeted with suspicion.

FAILURE IN PARIS—RETURN TO THE BATTLEFIELD

After months of intense diplomatic activity, an international conference on Cambodia, chaired by France and Indonesia, was held in Paris between July

30 and Aug. 30, 1989. After a promising start, the conference ended in stalemate, with delegates deeply divided over the issue of the inclusion of the *Khmers Rouges* in any future Cambodian coalition government.

The *Khmers Rouges* and troops of the Phnom Penh regime both increased their military activities ahead of the Paris conference. The progress and the subsequent breakdown of the conference brought to the fore the issue of the military balance in Cambodia following Vietnam's withdrawal in September. Although it was widely accepted that the troops of the Phnom Penh regime were no substitute for their Vietnamese allies, few commentators were prepared to predict that the *Khmers Rouges* had the strength to launch a successful onslaught after the Vietnamese pull-out.

A report in the *Far Eastern Economic Review* of Aug. 10 claimed that Phnom Penh troops had recently injured the *Khmer Rouge* leader Ieng Sary during a successful attack on a rebel command post at Khao Phlu in Thailand's Trat province. The report also claimed that the *Khmers Rouges* had recently launched "their heaviest-ever artillery bombardment" during an attack on garrisons in Battambang province. The escalation meant that the security situation along the Thai-Cambodian border—the principal battlefront—deteriorated sharply during July and August, and large numbers of refugees were forced to escape heavy shelling.

The first ministerial session of the international conference was held between July 30 and Aug. 1. The session was attended by Hun Sen, Son Sann and Khieu Samphan seated together as the "Cambodian" delegation. Other delegations were from Vietnam, Laos, Japan, Canada, Australia, India and Zimbabwe (the latter representing the Non-Aligned Movement) as well as the five permanent UN Security Council members (China, the Soviet Union, the USA, Britain and France) and the six ASEAN countries (Brunei, Indonesia, Malaysia, the Philippines, Singapore and Thailand). The Secretary General, Javier Pérez de Cuéllar, was also present.

The delegates agreed on July 31 to establish three "working committees" to prepare a draft document for approval by the conference in late August. In addition the conference also accepted a proposal made by Pérez de Cuéllar to send a UN fact-finding mission to Cambodia to gather "information of a purely technical nature".

The first committee, chaired by Canada and India, was set the task of drawing up ceasefire terms and defining the mandate of an effective "international control mechanism" to control the implementation of a settlement. A second committee, chaired by Laos and Malaysia, was set the task of defining guarantees for Cambodia's independence, sovereignty, territorial integrity and neutrality through the cessation of all foreign interference and external arms supplies and the prevention of the recurrence of "genocidal policies and practices". Australia and Japan were placed in control of a third committee to set out conditions for the return to Cambodia of the hundreds of thousands of Khmer refugees and to formulate the main elements of an international plan for the country's economic reconstruction.

In addition, a special *ad hoc* committee comprising France, Indonesia and the four Cambodian factions was established to examine the internal aspects of the conflict, namely the establishment of a four-party interim authority under Sihanouk's leadership and the organizing of internationally supervised elections.

A 15-member UN fact-finding mission, led by Lt.-Gen. Martin Vadset, the Norwegian chief of the UN Truce Supervision Organization, visited Cambodia and the Thai border on Aug. 8–17. The mission decided that a 6,000-strong force would be necessary to effectively supervise a ceasefire in Cambodia. Such a large force would be essential for a number of reasons, including the complexity of the military situation, the troublesome terrain and lack of infrastructure. However, an initial UN force of 150 would be enough to verify the Vietnamese troop withdrawal, which, according to announcements made in late July, would be completed by Sept. 27.

The various committees ended their deliberations on Aug. 28 having failed to formulate a draft agreement to place before foreign ministers returning to Paris for a final ministerial session starting that day. In the event the failure of the intense diplomatic activity embarked upon by the French and Indonesians to break the deadlock meant that a number of foreign ministers, including Shevardnadze, Baker, Major and Qian, did not return to Paris.

The level of participation of the *Khmers Rouges* in any future Cambodian government remained the main area of contention between the opposing Khmer factions and their respective patrons. Sihanouk and his supporters insisted that the incorporation of the *Khmers Rouges* into a future government was essential to avoid a prolonged civil war. Hun Sen, and his Vietnamese backers, maintained that the current *Khmer Rouge* leadership had no role to play in any future Cambodian regime. Both sides rejected a French power-sharing compromise put forward on Aug. 21. According to some reports, Hun Sen's refusal to compromise on the *Khmer Rouge* issue derived from a growing confidence in both Phnom Penh and Hanoi over the state of Cambodia's ability to withstand a *Khmer Rouge* onslaught after the Vietnamese withdrawal in September.

Another area of disagreement at the start of the second ministerial session on Aug. 28 was over the role of the UN in an international control mechanism. The Phnom Penh regime was generally wary of the mechanism coming under UN auspices, on the grounds that the UN General Assembly continued to maintain its recognition of the CGDK government.

There was also disagreement over the CGDK's demands that the issue of Vietnamese settlers in Cambodia be discussed. The *Khmers Rouges* claimed that the Vietnamese government had settled over 1,000,000 of its countrymen in Cambodia, an assertion denied by most independent commentators.

The conference was eventually suspended on Aug. 30 after delegates had adopted an anodyne final statement which noted that it was "not yet possible to achieve a comprehensive settlement". The statement said that France and Indonesia, as co-presidents of the conference, would begin fresh consultations with the participants within six months with a view to reconvening the conference.

Meanwhile, on the ground, all sides prepared for a fresh round of war . . . .

CHRONOLOGY

1st century A.D.   State of Funan founded in parts of modern day Cambodia and Vietnam.

6th century   Subjugation of Funan by State of Chenla.

800   Foundation of Angkor Empire by Jayavarman II.

1150   Completion of Angkor Wat at the end of the reign of Suryavarman II.

1444   Conquest of Angkor by neighbouring Ayutthaya.

1863   Protectorate treaty signed with France.

1887   Cambodia amalgamated into French dominated *Union indochinoise.*

1940   Japan occupies Indochina, leaving French colonial administration intact.

1941   French authorities place Norodom Sihanouk on the Cambodian throne.

1945   Japan displaces French colonial administration throughout Indochina; Sihanouk pressured into declaring Cambodian independence; Japanese surrender; Son Ngoc Thanh becomes Prime Minister; Re-establishment of French authority: Cambodia becomes "free state" within French Union; Thanh ordered into exile.

1946   Pro-Thanh Democrats win general election.

1947   First Constitution promulgated.

1950   Establishment of pro-Viet Minh United Issarak Front (UIF) led by Son Ngoc Minh; Minh declares Cambodia's "independence".

1951   General elections.

1952   Sihanouk dismisses government.

1953   Sihanouk abolishes National Assembly and orders arrest of large numbers of Democrats; embarks on "Royal Crusade for Independence"; Cambodia gains independence in November.

1954 Geneva Conference on Indochina accords international recognition to Sihanouk's government as sole legitimate authority within Cambodia; Communists begin to withdraw to North Vietnam.

1955 Formation of *Sangkum* by Sihanouk; Sihanouk abdicates to avoid constitutional restraints on his political activity; *Sangkum* wins massive victory in nationwide elections.

1956 Aid agreement with China.

1958 National Assembly elections; establishment of diplomatic relations with China.

1962 National Assembly elections and start of crackdown on the left.

1963 Pol Pot clique leave Phnom Penh for countryside.

1965 Sihanouk breaks off relations with USA.

1966 National Assembly elections: Appointment of Lon Nol as Prime Minister.

1967 Samlaut rebellion; Vietnamese communists begin to establish sanctuaries in eastern Cambodia.

1969 Nixon begins secret bombing of Cambodia (March); Lon Nol appointed Prime Minister for second term (August): re-establishment of diplomatic relations with USA; disappearance of Khieu Samphan *et al.* from Phnom Penh.

1970 Sihanouk overthrown by Lon Nol and Sirik Matak (March); joins forces with *Khmers Rouges*; American and South Vietnamese forces enter Cambodia in strength in April and May, and withdraw by late June.

1971 Lon Nol declares state of emergency (October); Republican forces suffer massive military defeat at Kompong Thom.

1972 Lon Nol dissolves Constituent Assembly, assumes the presidency and appoints Son Ngoc Thanh as Prime Minister (March); Presidential election won by Lon Nol (June); Social Republican Party wins all seats in general election (September); new government headed by Hang Thun Hak formed (October).

1973 Paris Agreements on ending Vietnam War signed (January); massive US bombing of Cambodia begins (February); In Tam appointed Prime Minister (May); secret 1969–70 bombing of Cambodia revealed (July); USA halts bombing of Cambodia (mid-August) in accordance with congressional prohibition; Long Boret forms new republican government (December).

1975 *Khmers Rouges* launch final offensive on Phnom Penh (January); overthrow of Lon Nol's republican regime (April) and establishment of *Khmer Rouge* rule; evacuation of Phnom Penh.

1976 Promulgation of Democratic Kampuchea constitution; appointment of Pol Pot as Prime Minister.

1977 Public emergence of Pol Pot as Communist Party leader.

1978 Full-scale attack by Pol Pot loyalists against So Phim's Eastern Zone dissidents. Leading survivors of Eastern Zone purge form "Cambodian National United Front for National Salvation" (CNUFNS) (early December); Vietnamese and CNUFNS forces advance into Cambodia (late December).

1979 Establishment of pro-Hanoi People's Republic of Kampuchea (PRK) headed by Heng Samrin (January); new government issues famine alert; invasion of northern Vietnam by Chinese troops (February and March); mass entry of Cambodian refugees into Thailand (April); Geneva Conference on Indochinese refugees (July); Cambodia's UN seat awarded to *Khmers Rouges* (September); West begins emergency food imports (October) after PRK agrees to allow border distribution.

1980 Vietnamese forces enter Thailand in pursuit of *Khmer Serei* guerrillas.

1981 PRK National Assembly elections and Kampuchean People's Revolutionary Party (KPRP) Congress (May); adoption of new Constitution and appointment of Pen Sovan, KPRP general secretary, as Prime Minister (June); UN-sponsored international conference on Cambodia held in New York (July); removal of Pen Sovan, Heng Samrin appointed new party leader (December).

1982 Chan Si appointed new PRK Premier (February); formation of rebel tripartite Coalition Government of Democratic Kampuchea (CGDK) (June).

1984 Start of successful Vietnamese–PRK dry-season offensive against CGDK forces along Thai border (October); death of Chan Si and appointment of Hun Sen as Premier (December).

1985 (August)   Vietnam announces intention to withdraw all forces from Cambodia by late 1990; fifth KPRP congress held (October), first Five-Year Plan adopted.

1986   CGDK issue "eight point" peace proposal (March).

1987   Hun Sen–Sihanouk meeting in France.

1988   Further Hun Sen–Sihanouk talks (January); first face-to-face talks between all the opposing Cambodian factions at Jakarta Informal Meeting (JIM 1) (July); adoption by UN General Assembly of revised "withdrawal" resolution (November).

1989   Hun Sen meets with Thai Premier Chatichai Choonhaven (January); joint Sino-Soviet nine-point communiqué on Cambodia issued; JIM 2 convenes (February); Vietnam announces (April) its decision to withdraw all forces from Cambodia by late September; Hun Sen–Sihanouk meeting in Jakarta (May); Pol Pot and Ta Mok resign from final *Khmer Rouge* posts (June); international conference on Cambodia held in Paris (July and August).

PART II:

REPORTAGE
EXPERT BRIEFINGS
REFERENCE SECTION

The wrecks of old cars help to shore up a new road (*David Munro/Oxfam*)

Garlic and smiles in a Phnom Penh market (*David Munro/Oxfam*)

REPORTAGE

THE STRAW POLL

John Pedler

As the Western powers were busy declaring in Paris that they supported Sihanouk's plan to give the *Khmers Rouges* a share of power in Cambodia—without first asking Cambodia's 8,000,000 people—it seemed to me a good idea to find out what a random group of Cambodians thought about the plan.

I realized from what I had already heard that I was embarking on an exercise in the absurd: to put it in Western terms, how does one ask a Jew if he would like the SS to share power in Israel? To ask such a question is in itself to give offence, to provoke—unless one can somehow exude such naivety that the respondent believes it necessary to give a serious answer. In other words it would be essential to my straw poll for me to appear to have no preconceived notion, being a foreigner quite ignorant of the country and its history. I decided to use two of my own friends as interpreters—a couple who live in penury because, as anti-communists, they cannot give support to the present regime and receive in turn the kind of senior posts that they might normally expect to get. With these assistants, I would be sure that no official interpreter came between me and my research.

My friend and his wife laughed at my proposed Western-style sociological investigation. But they well understood the reason for it since they are regular listeners to the BBC and had heard that Britain and America are behind Sihanouk and his "quadripartite" policy, which would have 10,000 *Khmer Rouge* troops in Phnom Penh as part of a four-faction army of 40,000. They saw right away that it was no use my returning to Europe and simply opining that the Cambodians would rather die at their posts than tolerate any return of the *Khmers Rouges*—I would need to ask at least 50 people before I could tell the media that my straw poll was *prima facie* proof that it would be grossly undemocratic, not to say immoral, to force the *Khmers Rouges* onto the Cambodians. They agreed with amusement to play the game of trying to present my enquiry as emanating from genuine ignorance so that I would not appear to be expecting the answer they well knew I would get. We would go somewhere, they suggested, where I could meet at leisure a good cross-section of society—rich and poor, townspeople and peasants. It would not be a scientific sample, but it would be more representative than many.

My friends secured the use of an aged jeep from a Chinese businessman for whom the husband did small jobs. It was Sunday. We drove 15 kilometres out of Phnom Penh on Route 1, the road to Saigon. There we turned off the road onto a well beaten track. In less than a kilometre we came to a riverside village of *paillottes*, the traditional Khmer thatched houses on stilts. Some were built out over the water. I had been there before with a film crew and was happy to go again. This was a weekend resort where cars and mopeds from Phnom Penh were parked in the shade of ancient trees. In the mainstreet, sitting crosslegged on their counters, sat hawkers of all manner of foodstuffs, cooked and uncooked. Youths and girls, in jeans and tee shirts—some with outlandish messages in English—wandered arm in arm sampling sweetmeats. English pop music blared. Further off in the village were the locals, *kramars* round their heads, watching "townee" ways intently, ready to let a room, or a fishing hut over the river, to a family for a picnic, or to lovers for love. A blind man was guided to a riverside hummock where the loudspeakers could hardly be heard. He began to play old Khmer tunes, wistful and sorrowful and burdened with nostalgia. Young and old gathered around. How intensely the Khmer enjoy their pleasures—they are few and simple and may never recur!

My friends got into conversation with townspeople and introduced me. I asked my question for the first time and got my first reply: "He would not ask that if he knew anything". It proved to be a frequent response. Others replied that though they didn't much like the government—for one reason or another—they were right behind it in refusing absolutely to do any deal with the *Khmers Rouges*. The peasants we talked to gave the same reply. Rather more of them than of the better educated seemed to be happy about Prince Sihanouk returning as Head of State, but only if he left the *Khmers Rouges* behind. I uncovered much fear on that day of rest and pleasure. Several I spoke to volunteered their own *Khmer Rouge* atrocity story. I could hear no more. I felt like a priest in the confessional, sick of hearing of sins.

I got up and walked to the riverside where my friends had taken a fisherman's straw hut for the afternoon. We sat down Khmer-style and ate charcoal-grilled fish, freshly caught from the river. Sleepily I watched long dugout canoes slide by, each loaded down to the gunwhales with a happy family. I heard the joyous shrieks of the children, the chatter of their elders wafted across the still water. Beyond were water meadows with cattle browsing, and beyond, as far as the eye could see, were flooded paddy fields patched with the bright green of newly transplanted rice. Interspersed were strips of market garden, growing for the Phnom Penh market.

"I think it's as near to heaven here as its possible to get", I remarked on impulse.

"Yes", said my friend's wife, "But hell is no further away than the water beneath us".

I looked down through the split bamboo floor at the water darkling in the shade of the hut. The opaque brown surface was scarcely a metre beneath. I wondered just how many convinced supporters of the *Khmers Rouges* there are among "the old people" in the wild hamlets of outer Cambodia. There are Nazis still in Germany.

1.   THE MILITARY BALANCE
Charles McGregor

Estimates of the strengths of the parties to the Cambodian conflict vary widely and much of the intelligence must be considered unreliable. Some of this may be blamed on such factors as biased and inflated refugee claims or the unsuitability of satellite reconnaissance in assessing the strength of small guerrilla units. More fundamentally, Western government analysts may be unintentionally distorting their interpretations of the intelligence. Western and South-East Asian policies towards the conflict are strongly influenced by their analysis of the military balance in Cambodia, but they are also affected by other important political considerations. There is therefore a danger that our information on the Cambodian military situation may to some extent be self-generated wishful thinking. Estimates of the number of men under arms are particularly suspect. While no analysis of the military balance could disregard such estimates, this chapter also puts emphasis on the assessment of recent fighting, force dispositions and declared strategy as factors that help indicate the military balance.

THE VIETNAMESE

In the months immediately before Vietnam's April 1989 self-imposed deadline for the withdrawal of all its troops from Cambodia, it was estimated to have between 50,000 and 70,000 troops still there, as compared to its peak strength of around 120,000. This was more than the State of Cambodia's regular armed forces and provincial forces combined, and it shows just how important the Vietnamese forces were to the security of the Phnom Penh regime. Until 1988, Vietnamese troops had done most of the front-line fighting. But after Vietnam's political initiatives had brought total withdrawal closer, its forces were gradually pulled back from the Thai–Cambodian border. Contrary to expectations, the security situation in Cambodia did not significantly deteriorate as Vietnamese troops began to pull back. Although they were still involved in front line combat, in particular by providing artillery support, the State of Cambodia forces that replaced them performed well.

The reasons for Vietnam's decision to withdraw its troops are complex, and encompass political, economic and military considerations. In military terms, there appear to have been two reasons for the decision to withdraw. First, Vietnamese troops had managed to control the military threat from the Cambodian resistance forces. The turning point was probably the 1984–85 dry season offensive, when Vietnamese forces managed to eliminate the opposition's camps on the Cambodian side of the Thai–Cambodian border. To some extent this gave the resistance forces greater freedom to operate an insurgency campaign from bases in Thailand, and to disrupt the Cambodian economy. While in 1986 and 1987 attempts to do so were made, they did not challenge the PRK's control of the provinces in which they took place. Efforts to restrict guerrilla movements across the border (under the K-5 plan), may have been an important element in preventing such operations. Lack of resolve on the part of the resistance forces to persist with such operations was also a major factor in encouraging Vietnamese withdrawal. From 1986–88 the resistance was relatively inactive, and it appears that Hanoi interpreted this as a sign of weakness. Moreover, while the resistance forces could use Thailand as their rear area, Hanoi's prospects for making any further headway in eliminating them were dim. Nevertheless, both Hanoi and Phnom Penh recognized that the *Khmers Rouges* still posed a threat. In such circumstances, withdrawal could not be a straightforward political decision. Military calculations must have played a major part in it.

There are three possible scenarios for Vietnam's withdrawal. First, given the unequivocal nature of its April 1989 announcement that it would unconditionally withdraw its troops by the following September, it would be difficult for Vietnam not to withdraw the majority of them, but the withdrawal might still be partial. The resistance factions and the Thai military have all expressed concerns that Vietnamese troops would remain in Cambodia "disguised" as State of Cambodia soldiers. If they remained as solely Vietnamese units, it is unlikely they would go undetected for long. However, it is difficult to see what particular benefit Hanoi would gain if Vietnamese troops were integrated into the State of Cambodia armed forces unless it was in such large numbers that, again, detection was highly likely.

Alternatively, Hanoi could keep several highly-mobile forces of regimental strength hidden in the Cambodian jungle, which could be called on to come quickly to the assistance of State of Cambodia forces in areas where they were particularly hard pressed by resistance forces. But once they came out of hiding, their presence would quickly be made known to the outside world.

For Hanoi, the difficulty with a partial withdrawal dressed up as total is that discovery might lose it both the moral advantage and accompanying political and economic benefits which it hopes for. So any Vietnamese force left behind in Cambodia would have to make a significant difference to be worth the risk. Yet the more impact it made, the more likely its presence would be detected. In sum, Hanoi is likely to have rejected partial withdrawal as a viable option, despite the *Khmer Rouge* threat, on the grounds that if the State of Cambodia's forces fail to cope, it could always re-intervene, in the meantime having benefited from international approval of its pull-out.

Re-intervention, the second possible withdrawal strategy, could take two forms. Complete re-intervention would take much the same form as the Vietnamese military presence over the past 10 years. It would probably be in politically more favourable circumstances; Hanoi might claim, with some justification, that its troops had withdrawn, but that the backers of the settlement had not controlled the *Khmers Rouges* and that it had been forced to intervene again for reasons of national security. It could argue that its willingness to withdraw had been proof that it did not wish to dominate Indochina. In the changing international climate in South-East Asia, Hanoi might hope that countries that had built up commercial relations with Vietnam and the State of Cambodia after Vietnam had withdrawn its troops would then be reluctant to isolate Vietnam yet again. In addition, Thailand might not be willing to allow its territory to be used as a rear area by the *Khmers Rouges*. The main argument against such a scenario is that the Soviet Union, which footed much of the bill for Vietnam's military presence from 1978 to 1989, would be unwilling to pay the costs of a renewed excursion. So complete re-intervention would have to be for a limited period, and there is little the Vietnamese could hope to accomplish in such an operation that they were not able to achieve in the 10 years of their first intervention. In the long term, Vietnam would also face mounting Khmer nationalist resentment of a Vietnamese military presence in Cambodia.

A second form of re-intervention would be limited to establishing a more defensible Vietnamese–Cambodian frontier against a prospective threat from resurgent *Khmers Rouges*. The most logical geographical boundary would be the Mekong River. While it would not be a barrier to small-scale guerrilla activity, it could be used to prevent large-scale insurgency requiring secure lines of supply. In political terms, however, such a strategy would make little sense. Western and South-East Asian countries would be unlikely to acquiesce in what would amount to Vietnamese annexation of Cambodian territory. It would compound the territorial grievances held by the Cambodian resistance with respect to the present frontier, further destabilizing the border area. Finally, it would not solve the long-term problem for Vietnam of an unfriendly country on its south-western border.

The third possible strategy for Vietnam is to withdraw entirely, with no intention of returning no matter what happens to Cambodia. In military terms, this means that it would be prepared for the security situation in Cambodia to deteriorate, even to the point of a resurgence of the *Khmers Rouges*. Vietnam would ensure its own security from such an eventuality by building up an effective defensive system along its border with Cambodia. There is already some evidence of it doing so. The planned restructuring of the Vietnamese armed forces, which emphasizes the role of the militia, thus giving them a defensive profile, together with a new emphasis on the primacy of economic policy over defence policy, all point to a decision in Hanoi to reduce its strategic links with the other Indochinese countries.

THE CGDK AS A MILITARY FORCE

The CGDK is primarily a political coalition. While its political unity has often been in question, the lack of military co-ordination between the National Army of Democratic Kampuchea (the *Khmers Rouges*), the *Armée Nationale Sihanoukienne* (ANS), and the Kampuchean People's National Liberation Army (KPNLA) has seldom been in doubt. The setting up of the High Council for National Defence by the CGDK in March 1989 to co-ordinate defence policy was simply a recognition of the coalition's weakness in that respect. It was an attempt to paper over the cracks and present a facade of military strength. It did nothing to dissipate the animosities that existed in the field between units of the various factions. Fighting between the *Khmers Rouges* and the ANS has been going on for a number of years; indeed, Prince Sihanouk gave it as a reason for his July 1988 resignation as president of the CGDK. There have also been intimations of fighting between the ANS and the KPNLF. As Vietnamese troops withdraw from border areas, the various CGDK factions may compete to establish control over the vacated territory. Indeed, such clashes between ANS and *Khmer Rouge* fighters were reported as early as mid-1988. The *Khmers Rouges* in particular have made clear that their ultimate goal is sole power. A 1986 document, purported to be a directive from the leadership to cadres, accuses the non-communist factions of collaborating with the *Khmer Rouge*'s enemies to "annihilate Democratic Kampuchea", and

as the document points out, "the *Khmer Rouge* is Democratic Kampuchea".
It continues:

> We have a firm concept. We stand by Democratic Kampuchea, which is our
> natural interest, because we really believe that there is no other alternative
> than Democratic Kampuchea which can protect your interest.

In 1988, *Khmer Rouge* guerrillas operating in Kompong Cham were reported
to be distributing leaflets vigorously condemning the Sihanoukist and KPNLF
factions. The resistance factions are unlikely to find the cohesion to launch
co-ordinated military operations. Given that military co-operation is unlikely,
an assessment of their strengths is therefore best done separately.

THE *KHMERS ROUGES*

The most widely used estimate of *Khmer Rouge* strength has been that it
has about 40,000 men under arms. However, some observers believe that the
positioning and equipment of *Khmer Rouge* units suggest that they are 40–60
per cent under strength. Some US intelligence estimates reportedly put the
Khmer Rouge's fighting strength as low as 20,000. Other Western sources
estimate *Khmer Rouge* fighting strength at about 18,000, with about 8,000
based around Site 8, some 5,000 in the north under Ta Mok and 4,000–5,000
under Son Sen in the south. Some observers believe the *Khmers Rouges* is not
a cohesive fighting force, and that there is competition between the military
leaders for power. But *Khmer Rouge* military operations on the border in 1988
suggest co-ordination between the various border sectors, even to the extent
of troops being moved to other sectors to take part in combined operations.
In June, the *Khmer Rouge*'s 519th division, based in the north-western border
area, moved south to support an attack on Phnom Milai by elements of the
320th and 450th divisions.

After the impressive performance of the Vietnamese in the 1984–85 dry
season offensive, *Khmer Rouge* fighters avoided contact with Vietnamese
troops. Together with the two non-communist resistance groups, it adopted
instead a strategy based on guerrilla insurgency, mainly against civilian targets.
The insurgency reached all provinces throughout Cambodia, including Kampot,
where the country's main port is located, Kompong Cham and Svay Rieng on the
border with Vietnam, and the provinces around Phnom Penh: Kandal, Takeo,
Kompong Chhnang, and Prey Veng. Yet despite this widespread insurgency,

the *Khmers Rouges* did not seriously challenge the political authority of the Phnom Penh regime in any province.

Aware that grassroots political support is a prerequisite of successful guerrilla warfare, the *Khmers Rouges* devoted more attention to political proselytization. Meanwhile, it stockpiled the weapons being supplied by China. It appears to have been creating a potential for rapid expansion. This now forms a key element in assessing *Khmer Rouge* strategic planning in the light of the anticipated withdrawal of Vietnamese troops.

A *Khmer Rouge* defector who had served under Ta Mok before joining ANS operations inside Cambodia estimated that the *Khmers Rouges* had stockpiled supplies to last for at least two years, and that in 1989 the *Khmers Rouges* had three guns for every soldier. His testimony should be treated with some scepticism, since the secretive nature of the *Khmer Rouge* organization makes it unlikely that anybody but the top leaders would be aware of the overall state of the group's supplies. Yet other defectors report taking part in a system for moving large quantities of arms from Thailand into Cambodia. US intelligence estimates *Khmer Rouge* stockpiles as sufficient for it to "sustain an active, low-level military operation for one to two years." China reportedly stepped up its arms supplies in late 1988, perhaps in response to the increasing likelihood of Thailand blocking distribution of arms through its territory in the event of a full Vietnamese withdrawal from Cambodia. State of Cambodia officials claim that two major *Khmer Rouge* arms caches have been discovered inside Cambodia in 1989.

By contrast, the *Khmers Rouges* have attributed their relative inactivity on the battlefield to shortages of weapons and ammunition caused by Vietnam's constriction of its supply lines, particularly at the border. By the same token, it has argued that since it could not supply the immediate needs of its fighters, it would have been impossible for it to build up arms stockpiles within Cambodia.

Even if the stockpiles are not as large as most estimates would have them, there is still some potential for re-supply. One possibility is re-supply by sea. The *Khmer Rouge* Command is reported to maintain logistics bases on at least one island in the Gulf of Thailand for supplies shipped from China. It might also attempt to gain a mainland seaport. Arms shipments would be vulnerable to interdiction, although Hanoi and Cambodia would undoubtedly be reluctant to become entangled in a naval confrontation with China. A more practical way of distributing Chinese aid to guerrilla forces might be in gold. Smuggling is endemic along Cambodia's borders, and there seems little reason to suppose that arms could not be bought, if the price was right.

The aspect of the *Khmer Rouge* capability to expand which is most open to question is that of manpower. In addition to its fighters, the *Khmer Rouges* controls some 50,000 Cambodian refugees. There are also an unknown number of Cambodian civilians without refugee status in secret *Khmer Rouge* camps in Thailand. Western diplomats say the number could be over 55,000, although estimates vary considerably, with some suggesting as many as 70,000–100,000. They constitute a reserve of manpower which the group draws on for fighters and for porters who supply its forward camps in Cambodia. In addition, they could be used to populate territory which the *Khmers Rouges* attempts to control within Cambodia. Similarly, territory which the *Khmers Rouges* capture and hold will provide it with further manpower resources. It seems doubtful whether the group's political proselytization would in itself attract supporters in sufficient numbers. Disaffected and bored youths in the refugee camps have become *Khmer Rouge* fighters for the excitement and status it provides. But the group relies primarily on fear to engender loyalty and co-operation. Once Vietnamese troops leave Cambodia, it will be much more difficult for the *Khmers Rouges* to appeal to Khmer nationalist sentiments, despite the links between Phnom Penh and Hanoi. Yet the efficacy of *Khmer Rouge* terror tactics in controlling large populations should not be under-estimated. After all, foreign intervention was needed in 1978 to end its rule of terror, and it has continued to control a large refugee population by similar methods.

Khmer Rouge strategic plans may be surmised as falling into three stages. First, the movement of *Khmer Rouge*-controlled populations in Thailand closer to the border, in preparation to cross back into Cambodia; a military offensive to retake camps lost in the 1984–85 dry season; and attempts to destabilize the State of Cambodia administration at the local level in the border areas. Second, the securing of defensible territory in the Cambodian periphery as a rear area for military operations, particularly if Thailand attempts to seal the border following the withdrawal of Vietnamese troops; the movement of *Khmer Rouge*-controlled populations into these areas; and the expansion of the *Khmer Rouge* army. Third, the launching of broad offensives to secure territory to provide the *Khmers Rouges* with an economic base. During these stages, there would be a parallel development of operations by *Khmer Rouge* units operating in the Cambodian interior, consisting of the consolidation of control over remote mountainous and jungle areas, the expansion of their fighting forces, the diversion of State of Cambodia military resources from the western part of the country, and the disruption of lines of communication and of supply lines from Vietnam.

The first stage of this strategy commenced in June 1988. The *Khmers Rouges* began moving some 7,000–8,000 Cambodians from the Ta Luan refugee camp in Thailand's Trat Province to assembly points near the border euphemistically called "repatriation villages". At the same time it launched a military campaign against State of Cambodia positions in the Thai–Cambodian border area, and attempted to retake bases just inside Cambodia. Fighting was especially heavy around Phnom Milai. Vietnamese reinforcements were brought up in August, causing the *Khmer Rouge* assault to falter, but throughout September, according to sources in Phnom Penh, State of Cambodia forces in the Thai border area were coming under heavy pressure in areas where the Vietnamese had withdrawn. By October, US intelligence indicated that the *Khmers Rouges* had accelerated its campaign to retake former bases, again with fierce fighting around Phnom Milai. Meanwhile, the *Khmers Rouges* closed O'Trao refugee camp in Thailand's Surin Province to Westerners, and moved an estimated 5,000–9,000 of its inmates to repatriation villages.

On this occasion, the *Khmers Rouges* acted prematurely. Vietnamese forces had withdrawn from the immediate border area, but reserves were still being kept in the border provinces for just such a contingency. Vietnamese troops intervened not only in the battle for Phnom Milai. In November, Vietnamese artillery units shelled the area around the O'Bok Pass in the Dangrek Mountains, forcing the *Khmers Rouges* to move the people in the repatriation camps back towards O'Trao. Other Vietnamese batteries in the south bombarded the refugees from Ta Luan. Vietnamese artillery units appear to have played an important part in denying the *Khmers Rouges* their objectives. By the end of the year, the *Khmer Rouge* offensive had abated.

Phnom Penh saw the fighting as decisive. Hun Sen claimed that "the *Khmer Rouge's* backbone was broken". While *Khmer Rouge* casualties were probably high, and the failure of the offensive undoubtedly dampened morale, the ensuing lull in *Khmer Rouge* activity was probably used to re-group and to bring fighting units up to strength. In January the PRK/State of Cambodia celebrated its 10th anniversary. *Khmer Rouge* units were reported to have threatened to disrupt the festivities. In the event, celebrations passed off almost undisturbed, leading Phnom Penh to claim that this was evidence of the decline of *Khmer Rouge* strength. Yet the *Khmer Rouge* units in a position to cause such disruption were not the units which had been involved in the border fighting in 1988. It seems more likely that, in the face of heightened security by State of Cambodia and Vietnamese forces during the festivities, the *Khmers Rouges* decided it would be an unwise time to mount an offensive, regardless of the propaganda value of successful attacks. Perhaps the failure of the group's premature 1988 border offensive had had a sobering effect on its leadership. Beginning in March 1989, the *Khmers Rouges* were reported to be moving refugees from its Borai Camp in Trat Province to repatriation camps. The move appears to have been prompted by UN Border Relief Operation (UNBRO) plans to relocate Borai's population to a new camp with greater international supervision. In an apparent attempt to weaken the morale of Phnom Penh's army, the *Khmers Rouges* launched intensive attacks on four Cambodian garrisons in Battambang Province in July 1989, reportedly using 130mm artillery.

THE NON-COMMUNIST RESISTANCE

The KPNLA ceased substantive military operations in 1987. It was paralyzed by a rift which appeared in December 1986 between the KPNLF leader, Son Sann, and the KPNLA's Commander-in-Chief, General Sak Suthsakhen. In the latter half of 1988, the KPNLF's Western and South-East Asian backers focused their attention on the lack of a credible military resistance other than the *Khmers Rouges* to fill an anticipated power vacuum as the likelihood grew of a Vietnamese withdrawal. They increased pressure on the KPNLF to settle its internal problems. While most of the field commanders appeared to side with Sak, others appeared to have recognized, by early 1989, that the group needed to reunify if it was to benefit from the West's desire to build up an alternative military resistance to the *Khmers Rouges*. In February 1989, Son Sann announced that he had received a request by KPNLA commanders asking him to become the Commander-in-Chief once again, and that he had accepted. Reports of engagements involving KPNLA units have since increased. Nevertheless, the strength of the KPNLA's unity remains open to question. In an effort to make up for the declining troop strength during the period of the rift, a concerted recruitment drive was launched in the last months of 1988. This succeeded in boosting numbers of men under arms from some 10,000 in mid-1988 to approximately 14,000 a year later.

A similar recruitment drive was conducted at the same time by the ANS, which claimed to have 21,000 combatants in mid-1989, double its strength a year earlier. As with the KPNLA, the ANS recruitment drive was mounted at the instigation of its Western and South-East Asian backers. Sihanouk travelled to Washington in October 1988 to seek backing for an expansion of the ANS. Progress was marred by allegations that some Thais responsible for distribution of earlier US aid to the non-communist factions had skimmed off some of the funding. This scandal, together with US budgetary constraints, led to the aid programme for fiscal year 1989 being cut from US$12,000,000 to US$8,000,000. US action to help expand the ANS was slowed due to the transition from the Reagan administration to the Bush administration. It was not until June 1989 that the White House launched a programme of covert aid, perhaps as much as US$30,000,000, aimed at increasing the strength of the non-communist factions to 46,000 by the end of the year. Meanwhile, the ASEAN countries were reported to be stepping up a secret training programme for the non-communist groups, with the aim of adding some 1,000 trained fighters per month to each of the two factions. While the goal was to provide an alternative credible resistance force to the *Khmers Rouges*, the long-term implications of a strong non-communist resistance force are not clear. The timetable for the expansion programme appears too optimistic. The non-communist resistance groups will have to react immediately to the Vietnamese withdrawal if they want to secure suitable strategic strongholds within Cambodia, otherwise the *Khmers Rouges* may beat them to it. The strengthening of the non-communist groups will increase the likelihood of clashes with the *Khmers Rouges* and perhaps even among themselves, because their respective areas of operations will increase. The dilemma facing the West and ASEAN countries is that in countering the *Khmers Rouges* by building up the non-communist forces, they may actually neutralize the Cambodian resistance.

With the withdrawal of the Vietnamese and the absence of a political settlement, the complete alignment of the resistance may be thrown into question. It is not clear whether either Sihanouk or Son Sann are prepared to countenance civil war without any prospect of winning in sight. If fighting settles into a stalemate once again, they may be tempted to realign themselves, with obvious implications for the military balance. Sihanouk in particular has long played with the idea of a settlement between his group and the Phnom Penh regime. There were reports in 1986 and 1987 that ANS and State of Cambodia units in some parts of western Cambodia were living under a *de facto* truce. In March 1988 Prince Ranaridh, C-in-C of the ANS, confirmed that elements of the State of Cambodia forces were "assisting", and providing them with supplies. Sihanouk even publicly called on his forces to strengthen relations with such units. Although that co-operation appeared to have broken down by the second half of 1988, with the ANS apparently going onto the offensive, it does demonstrate that the alignment of the resistance forces can become very vague.

Perhaps one of the most pressing questions for backers of the non-communist resistance is the position of Thailand with regard to its role as a conduit for supplies to the resistance once Vietnamese troops have withdrawn from Cambodia. It is unclear whether Thailand will stop the flow of military aid. In April 1989, Thailand's Prime Minister Chatichai was reported as saying that Bangkok had agreed that military assistance would be halted if there was both a cease-fire *and* a four-faction government under the leadership of

Sihanouk. The following month, questioned about a Vietnamese withdrawal, he confirmed that Thailand would halt its support for the resistance conditional upon the Vietnamese pull-out. He reiterated his proposals for a cease-fire and an International Control Mechanism, but apparently made no mention of a settlement between the Cambodian parties to the conflict as a necessary condition for the cessation of support.

While most ASEAN and Western countries might support Thailand in blocking aid to the *Khmers Rouges*, Bangkok might receive a less enthusiastic response if its policy were to affect aid to the non-communist resistance groups. If those groups had their aid choked off, they would have no stockpiles to fall back on—unlike the *Khmers Rouges*. The most valuable asset for the ANS in enlisting support within Cambodia will continue to be the strong, unquestioning loyalty of many peasants to Sihanouk. While State of Cambodia propaganda has succeeded in discrediting him with some peasants, an underlying fealty to the Prince may still exist in the countryside. Sihanouk himself is confident that there is a base of support inside Cambodia.

THE STATE OF CAMBODIA ARMED FORCES

The State of Cambodia's armed forces are divided up into three main sections: the **regular army**, the **regional** (or provincial) **forces**, and the **militia** (*Sena Chun*). Estimates of strengths may be wide of the mark because information is so scarce.

Most Western and ASEAN analysts agree that the **regular army** has some 40,000–45,000 soldiers under arms. The State of Cambodia Defence Minister, Tie Ban, is reported to have said that Phnom Penh's economic policies dictated that it would grow no larger, and Hun Sen also indicated that the main restraint on expansion of the regular army was economic. The regular army faced the brunt of the fighting in the border area as Vietnamese troops pulled back.

State of Cambodia **regional forces** number some 25,000. They are made up of standing battalions recruited and assigned at the provincial level, including companies assigned to districts and platoons in some sub-districts. However, in May 1989 an editorial in the KPRP newspaper *Pracheachon* stressed that the withdrawal of Vietnamese troops meant that regional forces had to "defend the motherland's border like the regular army". They would be rotated through the border areas for clearly set periods. Implying that regional battalions were under strength, the editorial called on provincial party committees and military commands "to implement the task of organizing forces . . . so that they are fully staffed and have reserve troops." It is possible that this will affect the morale of regional forces. One of the main causes of desertion has been that soldiers did not want to serve away from home.

Phnom Penh claims that the **militia** has been rapidly expanded by the simple expedient of arming the peasantry. From its claims that it now has 500,000 people under arms, it could be deduced that the militia now numbers over 400,000. While some Western analysts put the combined total of provincial and militia forces as low as 50,000, this is almost certainly an under-estimate; 100,000 militiamen is probably a more accurate figure. Political and economic reforms that took place in Cambodia in the first half of 1989 gave peasants land and greater freedom in production and marketing. They were intended to give those people a vested interest in the survival of the Phnom Penh regime. Arming the rural population was a logical, if somewhat risky, extension of that policy. In December 1988, Hun Sen admitted that the government was finding difficulty arming all militiamen with some possessing only "traditional weapons". From late 1988, however, an increasing number of peasants were issued with a rifle. Their greatest weakness may be a shortage of ammunition. Eastern European and Soviet diplomats have reported that militiamen are often forced to buy ammunition from the army, and even from the *Khmers Rouges*.

Phnom Penh's strategy for fighting the conflict by itself is divided into two parts. The militia's prime responsibility is to counter the small units of 10 to 20 guerrillas, particularly *Khmers Rouges*, who operate hit-and-run attacks in remote rural regions and on infrastructure in many parts of the country. Their job is primarily to deny the guerrillas shelter, supplies and food, while protecting their own villages and land. This makes the militia highly motivated. However, they lack training, and their discipline in combat must be open to question. The other facet of Phnom Penh's strategy is to contain the resistance forces on the country's northern and western borders. The willingness to re-designate regional troops to the border is evidence of the importance placed on this.

The fighting on the border looks set to develop into a number of static battles over territory. In such a situation, artillery will play an important role. In July, the *Khmers Rouges* were reported to have used 130mm guns, but it still relies heavily on mortar fire to support its infantry. The extent of the State of Cambodia's artillery is not clear. As late as mid-1989, it appeared still to be relying on Vietnamese artillery back-up, although at least one Cambodian battery had been observed. Much will depend on how generous the Vietnamese are in leaving behind their own artillery when they withdraw. Equally important, the State of Cambodia will have to rely on Vietnam and the Soviet Union for continuing supplies of ammunition for their guns. Air power, which played such an important role in Afghanistan after the Soviet withdrawal, is not a major weapon in Phnom Penh's arsenal. Its combat aircraft, a squadron of MiG-21 fighters, returned to Cambodia in June 1989, having spent the majority of the conflict based in Vietnam. Phnom Penh has said they will not be used in the conflict. It has no armed helicopters.

When the announcement was made in May 1988 that 50,000 Vietnamese troops were to be withdrawn from Cambodia that year, morale in the State of Cambodia armed forces was low. Up until that point, they had not been a major factor in front-line combat operations. Phnom Penh displayed uncertainty over its troops' ability to defend the country alone against the *Khmers Rouges*. The following year saw a remarkable change in attitude. By mid-1989 confidence was being expressed by the leadership and by soldiers of the Phnom Penh regime in their ability to tackle the *Khmers Rouges*. Phnom Penh claimed that the *Khmers Rouges* were under strength, that its morale was low, and that if outside aid to it were halted, the State of Cambodia's forces could manage to contain the *Khmer Rouge* danger. This was a promising development for Phnom Penh, inasmuch as the morale of the armed forces had been one of the main concerns about its ability to match the *Khmers Rouges*. It raises the question, though, of whether there was any substantive reason for the increase in confidence.

During the 1988 *Khmer Rouge* offensive, State of Cambodia regular and provincial forces had to be reinforced with Vietnamese troops. In particular, they relied heavily on Vietnamese artillery. In April 1989 further heavy shelling in the southern sector of the Thai–Cambodian border forced back *Khmer Rouge*-controlled refugees towards Ta Luan. It is not clear whether the action was by Vietnamese batteries or by new State of Cambodia artillery units. Phnom Penh claims this was combined with a major offensive against *Khmer Rouge* forces in the western sector of the Cardamom Mountains which caused the guerrillas heavy losses in men and equipment. Much of the improvement in KPRAF morale appears to have derived from this operation. Yet Phnom Penh showed signs of lack of confidence in its own strategy of containing the *Khmers Rouges*. In late June or early August 1989, in what was apparently a defensive move, it withdrew three crack brigades from the border, putting a greater burden on militia and provincial forces in the border region.

Reliable re-supply of military equipment and ammunition will be essential for Phnom Penh to effectively pursue its war against the resistance. This will ultimately come from Moscow. Vietnam will be unable to spare such resources, and will act as little more than a middle man. In the short term, the Kremlin will probably be generous. But it will want to see the stalemate broken. Phnom Penh recognizes that sporadic conflict with the guerrillas will be difficult to end on the battlefield. Publicly, it is optimistic that the scale of that conflict will not increase greatly following the Vietnamese withdrawal. If the fighting were on a much larger scale, with little prospect of Phnom Penh winning outright, Moscow might question whether the political and strategic value of Cambodia was worth the cost.

2. ECONOMICS, DEVELOPMENT AND AID

Frances D'Souza

INTRODUCTION

There are crowded restaurants in Phnom Penh; the city teems with bicycles and even cars. Small video cinemas have opened and the markets are full with locally-produced and imported goods ranging from thermos flasks and materials to toys. The predominant impression is one of bustle and optimism. This is an astonishing change from the desolation of October 1979 when the first observers reported on the ghost town of Phnom Penh and predicted that a further million would die by the Christmas of that year unless heroic emergency relief efforts were made. The response to Cambodia's horror was, if not immediate, generous in the short term. Over US$500,000 million was pledged to a beleagured country and more than 20 aid agencies eventually gained permission to carry out emergency programmes and some limited development. It was never easy; the restrictions were perhaps greater than in most emergency contexts; not the least being that Cambodia had lost its infrastructure. The problems that this posed are almost inconceivable. How was one to off-load vital emergency supplies at a port which had not seen service for perhaps 10 years? How could supplies be trucked to those in most need when there was neither transport nor viable roads? How could one set up a fair and free distribution system when village life was still in a shocked and suspended state?

Cambodia has come a long way, despite the severe isolation imposed upon it by major bi-lateral aid donors during the last decade. There is now the promise of a *détente* in Western attitudes to the country and its government, and in particular a keen interest in development programmes. Choices will have to be made, and although it is no longer true to say that Cambodia is a *tabula rasa* for the development experts, the kind of aid programmes agreed on will have profound effects on the people, the economy and on political stability. Cambodia has been the victim of international jostling for political position since the 1960s, as other contributions to this book demonstrate. Its history is one of colonization, wars of freedom, border skirmishes and exploitation by neighbouring states. The realistic fear is that this will continue, this time under the guise of binding, and ultimately exploitative, aid agreements. This chapter looks at what appears to be needed in Cambodia, and at the opportunities and constraints associated with different categories of aid.

CAMBODIA'S DEVELOPMENT NEEDS

The overall needs in Cambodia are, of course, similar to those in any developing country. They include an increase in agricultural production, the provision of health and education services, and an emphasis on income generation projects. On top of this, Cambodia also has special needs imposed by both its very limited resource base and in particular by the extraordinary constraints brought about through 20 years of war. The dislocation of people and the destruction of farming during the Pol Pot period are the two factors which have most contributed to Cambodia's poverty. These distressing conditions have been exacerbated by the refusal on the part of the UN and major bi-lateral donors to supply Cambodia with the massive amount of aid it needs in order to recover.

The conventional wisdom is that Cambodia is primarily an agricultural economy with abundant and fertile land. Cambodia was the rice-bowl of South-East Asia, it was confidently said. However, better informed sources point out that even before the devastation brought about by modern warfare and the Pol Pot regime, the economy was largely a subsistence one fighting a battle with uncertain rainfall and inadequate irrigation systems. Furthermore there is, and always has been, a clear division between town and rural life—so deep that the animosity between the two sectors of the population resulted in acts of gross brutality. It is not, and never has been, an integrated economy, and the incipient industrialization has depended to a very large extent on foreign (mainly Vietnamese) labour and investment.

Agriculture

Agricultural production has degenerated steadily in the last 20 years. In the late 1960s for example, it is estimated that approximately 2.4 million hectares were under rice, whereas by 1979 only 700,000 hectares were productive.

Similarly, the "yield percentage" of production per hectare dropped in the same period from 62.5 per cent to 40.7 per cent. In 1979 Cambodia's rice production was the equivalent of the food aid received by the Lon Nol government in 1974—280,000 tonnes. Since 1979 however there has been an astonishing degree of recovery. Thus, by 1989 rice production was officially estimated at 2.7 million tonnes although there is still an estimated 50,000 tonne shortfall. The improvement in production is attributable to at least three factors: the relative degree of stability since the ousting of Pol Pot; favourable seasonable rains; and the abandoning of the collective farming system in favour of private or family farming.

To some extent, relief and development programmes have also contributed to the improvement in agricultural production. Certainly the emergency provision of seeds and implements in 1979–80 was essential for rebuilding devastated land and irrigation systems. Larger aid programmes or those which are rooted in high-technology have, however, proved less successful. For example, there is a long-standing scheme to build a massive dam across the Mekong River between Thailand and Laos at Pa Mong. The principal objective of this scheme, master-minded by the Mekong Secretariat based in Bangkok, is the production of hydro-electricity, but the effect will be to reduce the extent and duration of the annual flooding surrounding the central *Tonle Sap* lake by at least 15 per cent. This would have very serious implications for the large percentage of population who inhabit this central area because of its fertility and abundance of fish. A further example concerns the high yield, "green revolution"-type rice seed (IR36) which may not be appropriate for Cambodia simply because the country cannot afford to import energy-intensive inputs essential to "green revolution" technology and does not have the resources to manufacture them.

As is the case in most developing countries, the need is for support and enhancement of local methods of food production relying on local resources, with a far greater investment in agricultural extension services in those more arid areas which are forced to rely on single seasonal crops.

Health and nutrition

Cambodia is one of the few countries in the world which is unlikely to achieve even the modest innoculation coverage for 1988–89 as laid down by the World Health Organization. This is a clear indicator of the weakness in the country's health infrastructure. By comparison, Vietnam, a country with great poverty and a far higher population density, is expected to exceed its own targets over the same period. Cambodia's health needs are immense and are compounded by two additional factors. Firstly, the obliteration of any kind of primary health care infrastructure during the Pol Pot years, including the reduction of trained Cambodian doctors from 450 in 1975 to 45 in 1979, has left the country virtually without any kind of health system. Secondly, the hatred and suspicion of anything but high-technology Western medical care due to the *Khmers Rouges*'s appalling efforts to outlaw treatment other than local methods, has made it extremely difficult to rebuild a medical system from the bottom up. Aid workers in the refugee camps on the Thai–Cambodian borders have had great difficulty in introducing primary health care based on paramedics and barefoot doctors for the same reason.

It is, however, not feasible to immediately institute a nationwide, high-technology, medical system. Of the 45 doctors remaining in Cambodia at the time of the Vietnamese invasion in 1979, 20 have since left, while of the 3,400 medical students only 728 have returned to Cambodia in the last 10 years. In all developing countries heavy reliance is put upon trained primary health care workers who can provide village-based health care cost effectively. The benefits are seen not only in improved child survival but in the establishment of country-wide networks vital for the introduction of other skills such as the training of more specialized health workers and the monitoring of health at village level. In association with aid agencies, the Cambodian government has introduced a system of RINEs (re-hydration, innoculation, nutrition and education) in several provincial towns and in Phnom Penh itself. These are apparently successfully run but it must be pointed out that since they concentrate on towns and cities alone they by-pass the majority of the population which is now based in rural areas. Other projects include efforts to improve water quality by the introduction of wells and education on basic hygiene.

Similar efforts have been made in the veterinary field although it will take many years to rebuild a sufficient and healthy livestock population.

Education and Training

Education is a further area which has shown remarkable improvement in the last decade. People have been prepared to build their own primary schools and in a population of a little over 7,000,000 the primary school enrolment exceeds 1,500,000 which is comparable to 1969, the last pre-war year of education. This achievement is perhaps more remarkable than it seems: of the 22,000 teachers in the country at the beginning of 1970, only 7,000 remained in 1979 and only 5,000 of these returned subsequently to teaching. Since then, however, more than 50,000 teachers have been trained or re-trained in the new centres located in each province. There remains nevertheless a major gap in the teaching of higher, professional and technical education, the major obstacle being the lack of qualified teachers. The government has made tremendous efforts to reduce illiteracy in Cambodia and in 1987 a figure of 83 per cent functional literacy was claimed. This was accomplished through two massive campaigns involving not only the teacher-training bodies but other peoples' organizations such as women's associations and trade unions.

Income generation and marketing

The basis for income generation in an agricultural society lies in the production of surpluses. It is only with surpluses that the individual can begin to trade. Although surpluses are being produced in Cambodia, to judge by the increase in food production generally, the benefit to the individual is hampered by at least three factors: (i) the lack of a developed marketing infrastructure to encourage trade beyond village-to-village level; (ii) the as yet poor prices paid by the government for agricultural produce, and (iii) the relative lack of consumer items, which normally act as incentives for farmers. Simply put, in a devastated economy a conservative farmer is unlikely to risk cultivating more than his carefully calculated needs for the coming year unless he can be sure that he will receive competitive recompense and/or is able to buy essential consumer goods such as soap, clothing, sugar and salt. This is a vicious circle, and experience in other beleagured countries suggests that the first step out of the impasse is to ensure the regular and widespread supply of consumer items. This in itself would help develop channels of local trade, from which would develop a marketing network and income generation.

Social and cultural considerations

Cambodia's needs, however urgent they continue to be, must be seen within a social and cultural context. There is thus a further major consideration to be borne in mind when deciding what forms of development aid are appropriate. This concerns the extent to which aid of whichever kind can unite social and cultural groups or act as a further barrier to the already considerable cultural alienation in the country.

Cambodia for centuries was a deeply divided society, so much so that communication between separate groups, such as the Khmer and others, was non-existent except for hostile and even brutal encounters. This separation of ethnic and other groups coalesced in the nineteenth century into an overt split between town and country. Crudely put, the towns held the élite, the court followers and the highly-educated, whereas the country was composed largely of small subsistence cultivators where even village organization and identity was weak. In the last 20 years town dwellers were also the rich who built Western-style villas and exuded other trappings of an international style of living. This expensive life was only possible by gross and sustained exploitation of the surrounding countryside and its agricultural produce. Peasants were required to provide the town with a percentage of each harvest and all with taxes. Vickery (1987) describes the ugly examples of an élite travelling group arriving at a village and demanding as of right a full meal including slaughter of a highly-prized chicken. The early policies of Pol Pot made explicit reference to this exploitation. His peremptory, albeit brutal solution, of the forced dispersal of people from the town and particularly harsh treatment of the "intellectuals" i.e. the soft élite town-dwellers, was not initially unpopular with the peasantry.

It would be all too easy to foster the division between town and country through inappropriately targeted aid and also through inappropriate training and education which would again promote an effete class at the expense of more functional training badly needed to rebuild Cambodia's resource base.

In this context the plans to rebuild and rehabilitate Angkor Wat and to encourage tourism are clearly of religious and historic significance for Cambodians. However, given the decades of exploitation Cambodia has suffered from one colonial power after another and by entrepreneurs thereafter it would be infinitely preferable if the reconstruction projects could remain a *Cambodian* enterprise with funding and technical assistance from donors.

THE NEW ECONOMY: OPPORTUNITIES AND CONSTRAINTS

The original motive behind Pol Pot's liberation was to enable the rural poor to survive. When the *Khmers Rouges* entered Phnom Penh in 1975 they were greeted as saviours. Widespread and deep public anger at the exploitation and corruption following vast foreign investment in the late 1960s and early 1970s was one of the major reasons for the defeat of Lon Nol and his surrender to the *Khmers Rouges*. Thus foreign investment and industrialization were in themselves symbols of the separation of town and country and the hated dominance by the city élites.

Traditionally, this has always been controlled by the Chinese, Vietnamese and a few dominant Khmer families. Industry was virtually non-existent and the education system not designed to produce engineers or technicians—but arts graduates. It is fair to say that up to the time of Pol Pot the educational system was in tune with the demand for status and wealth. Because of the lack of more pragmatic skills and the concomitant lack of industry, migrants from the rural areas worked almost exclusively in service trades such as servants, waiters, tailors and the like. Following the 1965 bombings in eastern Cambodia and the vast influx of refugees to Phnom Penh it was estimated that 10 per cent of the country resided in the capital but even with this great manpower resource there was still no development of industry.

In the late 1960s and early 1970s diplomatic relations with the United States resumed in return for a more favourable attitude towards foreign investment. Subsequent US military and other aid programmes were deeply abused and corruption was rife. Misappropriation of funds was a ubiquitous practice, the most famous being the claims by the Cambodian military for non-existent army units.

Premier Hun Sen has initiated fundamental economic changes, with more in the pipeline. The most important of these concerns a radical departure from socialism and especially from collectivization and the adoption of a more capitalist approach to recovery. The most dramatic changes are seen in the private farming sector. Peasants have been granted either ownership of land or long leaseholds, the collective sector has been all but abandoned. This has resulted in an immediate increase in production according to government figures on the amount of surpluses for sale either to the state or privately.

In addition, Hun Sen has steadily cultivated foreign investment at competitive rates. In July 1989 a new agreement was signed whereby foreign companies could invest in Cambodian enterprises in three ways. Joint ventures with the Cambodian government; 100 per cent foreign owned ventures; and contract joint ventures in which the government and foreign companies co-operate to run a factory or hotel (see Hiebert, 1989).

Foreign companies would be free to repatriate profits after paying a 15 per cent tax and would be given guarantees against future nationalization of their investment. Since the beginning of 1989 there has been a steady stream of foreign businessmen from Japanese, Thai, Singaporean and UK companies. Predominant interests lie in construction, industrial and manufacturing ventures, tourism and timber. The Australian Overseas Telecommunications Corporation has recently signed a Memorandum of Understanding with the government to install an earth satellite in 1990 which will greatly improve telephone links within the country.

Although much of this potential development awaits a political settlement it seems likely that some proposed projects will go ahead. There are opportunities and constraints. While Cambodia clearly has a need for investment on this kind of scale, its experience of foreign investment has not been an altogether happy one.

Thus, on the one hand, there are plans afoot to provide major capital investment for huge profit-making enterprises and at the other end of the scale there is so-called humanitarian assistance run mainly by a non-governmental organization consortium and two UN agencies which between them spend between $10,000,000–20,000,000 per year. This is a pathetically small amount of money given Cambodia's needs and one could argue that the Cambodian government's new overtures to foreign investors is partly a response to the West's persistent refusal to provide bi-lateral assistance.

There remains a huge gap, even if the proposed investment programmes are realized. The danger is that the economy will once again become top-heavy with a few favoured regions, including the main cities, as the prime centres of wealth, while the rest of the country will be forced to continue to struggle for survival. The only way in which a balance can be achieved is through sustained and appropriate investment in the agricultural base of the country. This requires not so much material aid as long-term programmes which involve training, agricultural extension projects, irrigation schemes and technical assistance in extending marketing networks. In addition, there is a clear need for investment in small-scale, even village-based, enterprises which are in themselves income-generating. These kind of projects would include workshops to both produce and repair agricultural machinery as well as manufacture bricks, other housing materials, piping for irrigation schemes, oil presses, and in time the production of school materials. These inputs are not only vital but also of the greatest urgency in view of the fact that a political settlement has not been achieved.

In a war context governments and aid agencies have the choice of not attempting any form of assistance until a degree of peace and stability has been achieved or providing life-saving aid where and when possible. However experience from other countries has led some agencies to consider different approaches. These concern the question of how one can run programmes that have some developmental ingredients despite the constant and severe disruption of internal conflict. The aim is to get away from continuous and expensive concentration on emergency aid. Such programmes are necessarily limited, but the major philosophy is to concentrate less on material inputs and rather more on assistance which will empower and enable communities to effect their own development. Thus the provision of agricultural implements for villagers, although a much-needed and excellent input, may have no lasting value if those implements have to be abandoned abruptly as fighting forces people to flee to distant areas of safety. However, providing training for agricultural extension work or for primary health care results in transportable skills. Training also meets the most basic gap in nearly all developing countries, and that is the dearth of skilled personnel in any kind of management expertise.

In the wake of the failure of the Paris talks, insecurity is a continuing fact, particularly in the north-west, and there are no guarantees that local conflict will be contained in the future. Investment is thus seen as a risky venture even by those agencies whose mandate is to work under the most arduous conditions. It has already been shown that one of the most tragic consequences of the Pol Pot regime was the depletion of the literate sector. Education of all kinds is perceived as a priority by both the government and the aid agencies, but so far relatively little has been planned let alone implemented on the technical level.

The second mechanism whereby people are empowered is through income generation. This is not necessarily to be seen as a simplistic approach along the lines of "let the people make money and they will at all costs protect their investment". Rather development is, or should be, concerned with increasing the individual's range of choices and this can best be achieved by extending his or her trading networks. This in turn is accomplished by ensuring that the individual has something to trade or exchange whether it be surplus produce, livestock or locally manufactured goods.

The twin goals of training and income generation are far easier to praise and discuss than they are to devise and implement. Nevertheless they must be attempted.

The country as a whole desperately needs income and yet Cambodia's natural resources do not lie in minerals or expanse of fertile land but in its history, its people and in its forests. Development of these assets is a distinct possibility, but the dangers of development becoming in the short and longer term a degradation of the land and remaining resources are ever-present. For example, world demand for timber is high and timber is one of Cambodia's few remaining valuable resources. Without stringent government controls it is entirely possible that large wooded areas will be rapidly denuded with disastrous environmental as well as economic consequences.

CONCLUSIONS

There are therefore priorities for development, and perhaps the guiding principles should be to concentrate on those inputs which will benefit the most impoverished as well as the largest section of the country's population. It has already been suggested that investment in urban-type projects cannot hope to empower the poor, economically or in any other way. The trickle-down theory of development has long been discredited, and in Cambodia it would be particularly difficult to invoke precisely because the articulation between rural communities and the larger urban centres was, and remains, extremely poor. The only hope therefore is to increase the natural resource base of the country and to ensure that the surpluses which will undoubtedly result from this investment can be distributed around the country to the benefit of the individual by substantial investment in transport and marketing. The golden rules for development in general, and Cambodia in particular, include the following:

a)   understanding the causes of poverty and under-development, which in Cambodia's case means meeting and ameliorating those conditions which prevailed prior to the Pol Pot regime;

b)   ensuring that aid does not, at the least, exacerbate the problems but instead addresses them;

c)   emphasising the role of all aid projects in enhancing the fit between population and resources rather than introduce new and unfamiliar technologies;

d)   understanding that development is primarily based on imparting technical skills to people at all levels, and in particular those skills which are transportable.

3. WAR OR PEACE?

John Pedler

Much of this chapter is subsumed in a sombre gem of Cambodian humour:

"Whatever's the matter with Vietnam?"
"Oh, it had the misfortune to win a war against the United States".
"Then, whatever's the matter with Cambodia?"
"Why, it had the misfortune to be liberated by Vietnam".

Since the collapse of the Paris Conference in July and August 1989, and the departure of the last Vietnamese troops in September, Cambodia has had to face up to the likelihood of all-out civil war—not only against the *Khmers Rouges*, but also against the less effective forces of both Prince Norodom Sihanouk and of Son San's KPNLF. Prime Minister Hun Sen believes that China and the United States together engineered this recourse to arms rather than accept the peaceful solution of the Cambodian problem that he had all but negotiated with Prince Sihanouk in two and a half years of talks. As the Paris Conference ended, the Cambodian government was obliged to recognize that—apart from the "Soviet bloc", including Vietnam—it has no friends it can count on, since there are few countries in the world that can stand up to the combined pressure of two superpowers over the same issue at the same time.

Why has this trial of armed strength come about? Why did peace talks fail? Can the recourse to arms be stopped or at least mitigated? What are the chances of survival for the defenders of Cambodia and its 8,000,000 inhabitants? Can the circumstances in which the struggle is fought out be so altered by some of the international community as to better these chances?

Answering these questions demands a brief look at the background uninfluenced by the propaganda of the *Khmers Rouges*, of Prince Sihanouk and of the "socialist" countries including Vietnam and the present regime in Cambodia. Propaganda by all sides, together with an absence of diplomatic reporting from Cambodia itself for 15 years (the result of the non-recognition policy and the boycotting of Cambodia by the West) has led to widespread misconceptions.

VIETNAM

Let us first quickly review the story from a Vietnamese perspective before considering the position of the other players.

Vietnam invaded Cambodia twice—in 1977–78 in a punitive expedition, and again in 1978–79 because—after much restraint—it could no longer endure the armed provocations of its erstwhile protégés, the *Khmers Rouges*. The Vietnamese themselves claim that the *Khmer Rouge* massacres and atrocities accounted for around 30,000 deaths on their side of the frontier. While this figure cannot in the nature of things be confirmed, reputable Western observers, such as Nayan Chanda of the *Far Eastern Economic Review*, have witnessed the appalling results of some of these attacks.

Much of the Cambodian–Vietnamese frontier, delineated by the French when both countries were in the French empire, is a frontier traced primarily from ethnic not strategic considerations. There is, for example, the so called "Parrot's Beak" where, as the Americans used to say, the Cambodian province of Svay Rieng "points like a dagger at Saigon". No-one responsible for the security of southern Vietnam can accept for long a Cambodia which is being used as a base against Vietnam. It was for this reason, when America was defending South Vietnam in the late '60s and early '70s, that the United States eventually decided to back General Lon Nol's *coup d'état* in 1970 which overthrew Prince Sihanouk, and then to invade Cambodia along with South Vietnamese forces. The plan was to cut frontier areas, and so to secure the South by control of eastern Cambodia. Instead, South Vietnam overextended its line of supply and was beaten in a battle that some consider the beginning of the end for the South. Cambodia and Laos are traps for conventional forces to avoid—it is a lesson that Vietnam, which taught it to America, had to relearn itself when, by one of history's quirks, roles were reversed and it was Vietnam's conventional force that was fighting the very guerrillas Vietnam itself had helped to power in Cambodia.

The *Khmers Rouges* were initially trained by the Vietnamese in the years following Dien Bien Phu and the independence of North Vietnam in 1954. At this time North Vietnam was engaged in its "rectifications" campaign which involved the mass killings of better-off peasants and other undesirable elements who were commonly required to dig their own graves before being shot into them. To some extent this followed precedents set by Stalin's Soviet Union, and, more recently, Mao's China. North Vietnam therefore merely followed suit after its own consolidation of power. General Vo Nguyen Giap eventually put an end to this because of the adverse effect on national morale at a time when he was stepping up the war against the South.

So *Khmer Rouge* mass slaughter after their takeover came as no surprise to the Vietnamese. The scale though, did eventually come to appear to them as excessive and counter-productive, for the same reasons that had led them to call off their own purge.

What led to the Vietnamese invasion was Pol Pot's military ambitions—specifically his irredentist territorial ambitions. As Sihanouk puts in in his essential memoir, *Prisonnier des Khmères Rouges* "The main motive for Pol Pot mounting . . . attacks by the best units of his army against Vietnam . . . was his frenetic desire to recover the lost provinces of the former Khmer Empire. Pol Pot believed himself to be . . . a more fortunate Hitler".[1]

Ironically, the Vietnamese found themselves hailed by the great majority of the Cambodian population as "liberators", when all they were doing was to take measures against the Pol Pot Frankenstein they themselves had helped to create and to imbue with their own strategies. They found themselves—to the credit of many individual Vietnamese and elements of the Vietnamese government—engaged in emergency humanitarian aid. They had to send rice supplies from their own limited stocks to starving Cambodians and mount a first aid plan to reconstruct a devastated country reduced to Pol Pot's terrible "Year Zero". Despite the immemorial antipathy between the Cambodians (very much the "Indo" side of the Indochina divide) and the Vietnamese (firmly on the "China" side), many Cambodians will long remember the humanitarian efforts of devoted Vietnamese—such as rescuing, caring for, and educating many of the thousands of orphans of Pol Pot's massacres. Nor of course do Cambodians forget that, in the face of one of the great genocides of the twentieth century, Western governments did virtually nothing whatever. What little has been contributed from the West comes from non-governmental organizations, sometimes in defiance of their home governments.

It was in the aftermath of utter destruction and "auto-genocide" that Vietnam set up the People's Republic of Kampuchea. Like the Allies in Germany, the Vietnamese cast around for capable individuals who could provide the skeleton of an administration amidst almost unparalleled destruction. For a nucleus, they found *Khmer Rouge* cadres who had fled to Vietnam or who had rebelled against the *Khmers Rouges* in Heng Samrin's Eastern Rebellion.

[1]Norodom Sihanouk (Hachette) 1986, p.207.

Like the Allies in Germany when they set up a Western-style democracy in place of the Nazi government, the Vietnamese created a government in their own image—in their case a government mirroring their communist regime in Hanoi. As in Germany, this government was initially heavily dependent on the advice of the occupation forces. In Germany, the Allies were constrained to take a large hand in government because so many qualified Germans had been implicated in Naziism. In Cambodia the Vietnamese role was magnified because Pol Pot had wiped out a majority of the administrative, intellectual, and technological class: there were not even enough communists to staff a skeleton government. From the first therefore, the Phnom Penh government was diluted by non-party cadres, even at the top of the pyramid. To take but one example, no other communist government would have appointed a strictly non-party man—Hor Nam Hong—as the Minister responsible for its most delicate negotiations (those with Sihanouk, Son San and the *Khmers Rouges*).

The burden on Vietnam was the greater because the West laid siege to Cambodia. Western governments did virtually nothing to alleviate the apalling sufferings of the Cambodian people: their argument was that any aid whatever to Cambodia helped take the burden off the Vietnamese in maintaining their occupation of Cambodia. The West and the Association of South East Asian Nations (ASEAN) withheld recognition to the Cambodian government, and not only refused all aid, but imposed an economic blockade on the country. A major effort was mounted by the US and China, helped by ASEAN and the rest of the West, to ensure that the *Khmers Rouges* kept their "Democratic Kampuchea" seated in the United Nations General Assembly: this was done by pressing Prince Sihanouk into being titular head of a Coalition Government of Democratic Kampuchea which existed only on paper. This stratagem conferred sufficient respectability on the *Khmers Rouges* to keep them in business as a government despite their loss of the national territory.

The West and ASEAN policy towards Cambodia was determined by the overriding concern at the presence on Thailand's frontier of the Vietnamese army—then assessed as the world's fourth largest and enjoying the unparalleled prestige of having not only beaten France but also of being the only one ever to have defeated the United States. These countries feared—not without reason as it seemed at the time—that the invasion of Cambodia could mark the beginning of a new phase of Vietnamese expansionism. It evoked the old American nightmare of the "domino theory" whereby communism would spread from Vietnam into one country after another right down to the islands off the north of Australia.

The evidence about Vietnamese intentions when they invaded Cambodia in 1979 is not conclusive. It is not yet possible to say whether Pol Pot's provocations of Vietnam re-awakened Vietnamese ambitions to control all French Indochina or whether this had been dismissed already by Hanoi as an impractical dream. Certainly in 1975 Vietnam was exhausted after winning its wars. What we know suggests that it had accepted the loss of Cambodia from its sphere of influence and was solely concerned to keep Laos within it. Vietnam apparently felt obliged to appease the Chinese backed *Khmer Rouge* regime: Sihanouk, for example,[2] cites 10,000 Cambodian refugees being handed back to Democratic Kampuchea by Vietnam.

Even after their invasion of Cambodia, the Vietnamese did not at first approach the Thai frontier in force. They contented themselves with holding the populated areas and leaving mountain and scrub to the guerrillas. It was renewed *Khmer Rouge* guerrilla activity after its partial reconstruction by China with US complicity, and the attendant Vietnamese casualties, which finally obliged Vietnam to mount its 1984–85 dry season campaign forcing the *Khmers Rouges* back to the Thai frontier. At the approach of General Douglas MacArthur's UN forces to their frontier in the Korean war, the Chinese believed a threat to China was imminent. In the same way, the arrival of Vietnamese forces in strength on the Thai frontier naturally enhanced the already grave suspicions of Vietnamese intentions.

It is quite likely though that the Vietnamese invasion of Cambodia in 1975 threatened no-one beyond Cambodia; that they had taken no firm decision to remain in military occupation. It is as probable that the Vietnamese were taken aback by the charnel pits of Pol Pot's "auto-genocide" and by the near total "auto-destruction" of the economy which obliged them to stay in Cambodia instead of simply to leave after replacing one group of leaders by others less bellicose towards Vietnam. It may plausibly be argued that it was the vacuum in Cambodia that obliged them, willy nilly, to prolong what was intended as a brief sojourn into a prolonged stay in order to re-establish from nothing some semblance of stability and competence in a regime that was to be their future neighbour.

Equally, it is as possible to argue that the Vietnamese stay in Cambodia was prolonged, not shortened, by the Sino-American success in reviving the defeated *Khmers Rouges* and in setting up a rebel "government" with Prince

[2]op. cit. p.187.

Sihanouk as its titular head. For how could Vietnam leave Cambodia when foreign powers had created a new, heavily armed *Khmers Rouges* designed to come straight back and continue its provocations of Vietnam where it had left off in 1978? That the USA was an accomplice to China over the *Khmers Rouges* has been admitted by President Carter's National Security Adviser, Zbigniew Brzezinski: "I encouraged the Chinese to support Pol Pot. I encouraged the Thais to help the Democratic Kampuchea . . . Pol Pot was an abomination. We could never support him but China could".[3] If the *Khmers Rouges* had been left simply as refugees in Thailand without arms from China and elsewhere, Vietnam's disengagement *could* have taken place years earlier than 1989. But as to whether it *would* have taken place cannot yet be known.

Vietnam did not leave Cambodia because of military defeat. Losses were comparatively low after the 1988 dry season campaign and could have been sustained for years. Even the costs of the occupation were not unacceptable for so important a purpose as securing the western marches of Vietnam's sphere of influence.

The Cambodians had become progressively less grateful for their deliverance from Pol Pot, and progressively less tolerant of the Vietnamese occupation. But again this was containable: Vietnamese forces had learned—like foreign forces in the two Germanies—to keep out of sight as much as possible. The discipline of the Vietnamese army kept Vietnam's reputation as an occupation force surprisingly high: there appear to have been remarkably few incidents of maltreatment of the Cambodian population—though excessively tough treatment was undoubtedly meted out in many cases to *Khmer Rouge* suspects. Off duty, as the writer has observed in reasonably secure provinces, Vietnamese troops were commonly unarmed and engaged in limited but congenial relations with the people—and (like GIs before them) particularly popular with the kids.

It was primarily economic considerations inside Vietnam itself which forced a reappraisal of the Vietnamese occupation. Vietnam's military prowess had not been matched by economic know-how. Its infrastructure and much of its industry largely destroyed by war, Vietnamese-style communist economics proved quite incapable of bringing about the vast reconstruction required to make Vietnam prosperous again. Perhaps even more important, the rise of population to 64,000,000 (Hanoi's figure, January 1989) demanded an exceptionally rapid advance to industrialization if living standards were to be maintained, let along raised—and that could not be achieved by the

---

[3]Elizabeth Becker, *When The War Was Over*, p.440.

bureaucratic processes of communism. Indeed, some economists doubt if it is any longer possible—even were there a free market economy and vast injections of foreign aid—to overtake the nemesis of a population explosion of almost the same urgency as China's. A Vietnamese Minister told the writer in Hanoi early in 1989, "It was no small struggle to defeat France and America to obtain our independence. But it will be an even greater struggle to defeat the population problem. Success is not assured".

It was not poverty itself that caused the Vietnamese withdrawal from Cambodia, but the effectiveness of the largely American-inspired economic boycott of Vietnam so long as it maintained troops in Cambodia. Without development funds Vietnam has no chance of beating its population problem—or even of renewing its infrastructure. The imperative for capital demands the end of the Western economic blockade which has been conditional upon the withdrawal of the troops from Cambodia.

Now that the decision is taken, the degree of disenchantment with the war has become apparent: "We Vietnamese are tired of helping those ungrateful Cambodians. I hope we never have to help them again" said one Vietnamese Ministry of Foreign Affairs official after meeting a particularly nationalistic Cambodian who, after the mildest and most polite of requests, had said peremptorily "I'm not taking orders from a Vietnamese". The Vietnamese official reflected quite a common sentiment. Many Vietnamese though are proud of their country's role (albeit accidental) in saving the Cambodians from *The Killing Fields*—a movie the writer was urged to see by Hanoi dissidents.

As the Vietnamese final withdrawal was taking place, US Assistant Secretary of State Richard Solomon took Vietnam to task for pulling its forces out and simply "walking away" without attempting to leave behind a political solution. This is not correct. The Vietnamese appreciated—at least from early 1987—that the corollary to their military departure was a political settlement. Their one requirement—understandably—was that there should be no return of the *Khmers Rouges*. The Soviet Union also wanted an end to the Vietnamese occupation: not simply to escape footing the bill but because Cambodia was a thorn of contention in Sino-Soviet relations. The Soviet Union additionally wanted an end to this regional conflagration as part of its world-wide policy of *détente*. No longer interested in communist expansionism, the Soviet Union was primarily concerned to preserve its gains from the Vietnam War: a friendly Vietnam and bases in its southern part.

Vietnam and the Soviets therefore accepted that the price of troop withdrawal was to permit Cambodia to leave the "socialist bloc" and go its own way as a stable, neutral buffer state between Vietnam and Thailand: something which had previously been acceptable to both China and the United States. The US Administration has not been prepared to give Vietnam credit for this. Indeed, Solomon's attitude partially justifies Cambodian Premier Hun Sen's remark to the writer in February 1989—"When we or Vietnam meet one US demand, the US simply makes another one".

When the Cambodian regime told Vietnam and the Soviet Union that it considered that the best hope of obtaining a swift and more or less total solution lay in Prince Sihanouk, these two powers acquiesced in direct negotiations between Hun Sen and the Prince. The first of these talks took place at a chateau near Fère-en-Tardenois, near Paris. The negotiations got off to a surprisingly hopeful start. Sihanouk's first remark was that Cambodia's terrible history had come about as a result of "the Americans who had me deposed in March 1970"[4]. Hun Sen replied that without the American intervention he would not have lost an eye fighting for the Prince.[5] This mutual expression of mistrust of the United States seems to have oiled the meeting, for the two men went on to agree the essentials of an accord. This embraced the return of the Prince as Head of State after breaking with the *Khmers Rouges* and the "decommunization" and "devietnamization" of Cambodia.

China, together with America, ASEAN, and other Western powers attempted to ensure a place for the *Khmers Rouges* in any new regime. Throughout, Hun Sen made it plain that there could be no return of armed *Khmers Rouges* if only because the overwhelming majority of Cambodians would not accept any return of their butchers. But as the discussions continued between the principals it became clear that the two sides would accept that the final agreement would be subject to two conditions: that the Hun Sen government should alter its communist-style constitution to clear the way for free, internationally-supervised elections; and that the Prince, for his part, would break his links with the *Khmers Rouges*.

By mid-July 1989 a draft agreement was on the table. The only matter of first importance left for Hun Sen and Sihanouk to determine themselves at their scheduled meeting in Paris on July 24 was exactly what the *Khmers Rouges* were to be offered in the period before elections. What was envisaged was a fourth share in some kind of supra-governmental authority which would determine the modalities of a general election. Both Vietnam and the Soviets

---

[4]op. cit. p.87.
[5]Hun Sen says he originally responded to a Sihanouk broadcast asking loyal Cambodians to join his resistance forces. He claims that when he joined the resistance, Sihanoukists were thin on the ground (in fact they were purged by the *Khmers Rouges*)—and that was how he found himself fighting with the *Khmers Rouges*.

concurred in all this: it is hard to imagine how either power could have done more to ensure a pacific transfer of Cambodia from the "socialist bloc" after the Vietnamese departure.

PRINCE NORODOM SIHANOUK

In 1941 Prince Sihanouk, a sensitive, intelligent youth with strong artistic leanings, was chosen to be Cambodia's new king under the French Protectorate. The French expected him to be a pliable and near powerless constitutional monarch. But he "grew on the job". It was he who demanded, and got, Cambodian independence from France in 1953. And it was he who persuaded guerrilla groups, such as that of "Dap" (Corporal) Chhuon Mochulpich, who had been fighting both French and Japanese, to rally to him, so bringing near total peace to the kingdom. In 1955 the Prince abdicated as king to avoid the constrictions of the constitution. He became the unquestioned ruler of the country until the *coup d'état* of 1970. For 15 years Cambodia enjoyed stable government and made remarkable economic progress—first reconstructing after France's Indochina war of 1945–55, and then building a post-colonial economy. Exports of rice (much of it in the hands of the prosperous Chinese community) and rubber (in the hands of a small group of French former "colons") provided adequate foreign exchange for what was still a mainly self-sufficient agricultural community of some 7,000,000 people.

Foreign policy was another matter. By about 1956 the Prince foresaw a further round of conflict in Vietnam where President Ngo Dinh Diem had been eased into power by the United States. Faced with the risk of the worsening "troubles" overflowing into Cambodia and consequent Thai concern, the Prince decided that he must bring communist China into the equation as a kind of guarantor against both Vietnam and Thailand, and as a counter to growing, pervasive American influence replacing, throughout Indochina, the former French presence. He therefore recognized communist China and began his astonishing tightrope act balancing rival pressures from Hanoi, Moscow, Saigon, Washington, Peking and Bangkok. In this delicate task he was advised by Prince Penn Nouth, an aristocrat with a professional understanding of diplomacy which balanced the Prince's own unorthodox, and at times uncertain, brilliance. Behind the Prince's much publicized "mercuriality"—his dramatic changes of stance—lay almost always cool calculation. A perceptive Soviet diplomat who knew the Prince in those days and who has watched his performance since, remarked to the writer, "In the '60s the Prince used his temperament to get what he wanted politically. In the '80s his temperament has destroyed his ability to realize his aims".

A number of factors weakened the Prince's regime so that it took but a light push to overthrow. First was the vast escalation of the war in South Vietnam. As mentioned already, the North Vietnamese used Lao and Cambodian territory for their famous "Ho Chi Minh" trail through the jungle and brousse to the west of the Annamite Hills chain to supply the Vietcong and their own forces in South Vietnam. They established a series of bases along the strategically delicate Vietnamese frontier which were used to great effect in the struggle against the Americans and their allies in South Vietnam. They became bolder and began shipping supplies through the brand new French built port of Sihanoukville (now Kompong Som). The Americans and South Vietnamese protested energetically, and because of this pressure the Prince flew via France to Moscow in the spring of 1970 to point out that a neutral Cambodia would not long survive unless Moscow put pressure on Hanoi to reduce the misuse of Cambodian territory. It was when the Prince was away on this mission that Lon Nol, left in charge, took over Cambodia for himself.

It would be a mistake though to explain Prince Sihanouk's downfall as being solely due to his fall from the diplomatic tightrope. The Prince himself had sent many young people to France for their education. They were dismayed when they returned with their Sorbonne degrees only to find that there was no room for them in the Prince's scheme of things because he himself insisted on deciding policy down to unimportant details. He could not delegate, he had to interfere. Because they knew more than he did and pointed this out, the Prince came to resent those he had himself nurtured intellectually. He came to mistrust them.

Peasant dissatisfaction began to grow particularly in the west: the Prince put down one demonstration savagely. The general malaise was fanned by the *Khmer Serei*—a left-leaning organization. The Prince dealt with this by shooting without trial some hundreds of dissidents and then forcing students and others to watch films made of the executions. Many Cambodian bourgeois tell you today how, as school children, they found these compulsory films obnoxious and frightening. They revealed another, sinister side to genial "Samdech Euv" as the Prince was affectionately known.

Perhaps even more damaging, corruption—always rampant in Cambodia— spiralled out of hand. The Prince's wife, Princess Monique was widely alleged to be at the centre of a major focus of corruption around the Prince's own family. When Prince Penn Nouth pointed out the political damage being caused by Monique's clique, they prevented him from having free access to the Prince. It was like removing the balancing pole from the tightrope artist. Ever more sucked in by the whirlwind of the Vietnam War, the Prince proved unable to cope on his own. As early as 1968 the writer was warned by Lao Prime Minister

Souvanna Phouma that unless something radical was done to stop the rot the Prince could not survive more than a year or two. Prophetically, Souvanna added—"As goes Cambodia, so goes Laos". The savagery of communism was to cover both of these countries, steeped in Hinayana Buddhism which, in important respects, were then more civilized in the basic sense of that word than the materialistic societies of the developed world.

The Prince was in Moscow when he was overthrown. The Soviets and the French offered an aircraft to go back to Phnom Penh—in the manner of Emperor Haile Selassie of Ethiopia when similarly deposed during his absence abroad. But the Prince chose to go to China—the country he relied on to redress the balance and preserve an independent Cambodia. There—as already noted—he made his radio appeals to his countrymen to join his resistance forces in the jungle, thereby unintentionally swelling the strength of his old enemies, now brusquely turned allies, the *Khmers Rouges*. So began—partly as a result of his own mistakes, and partly as a result of US policy, Prince Norodom Sihanouk's cohabitation with his *Khmer Rouge* enemies which still continues today after one and a half decades: the same length of time as he ruled Cambodia with considerable success as a—largely—benevolent despot.

At the time of Lon Nol's *coup d'état* the *Khmers Rouges* were still a small Vietnamese-trained group of no grave significance. Their numbers were very soon much increased by the Prince's overthrow and Lon Nol's campaign to destroy opposition in the countryside. They were also increased by those who rallied to Sihanouk—for the Sihanouk guerrillas were sparse on the ground and ill-equipped. Hun Sen, the future prime minister of Cambodia, was far from alone in discovering that volunteering for the Prince in effect meant fighting for the *Khmers Rouges*. Massive American bombing[6] acted—as American air power had already done in Vietnam—as a powerful recruiting sergeant. The Lon Nol regime's violence, and its degree of corruption (now large American funds were available) exceeded anything under Sihanouk, and led to ever-growing alienation of government from people. A gulf grew between the peasants and countryfolk who underwent ruthless Lon Nol "search and destroy" operations as well as the B52 carpet bombing—and those in Phnom Penh and the provincial towns who lived well, but often decadently, and whose chief fear was of serving in Lon Nol's army. This division led to the formation of two nations under the *Khmers Rouges*: the "old people" who had been with—or under—*Angkar* in the Lon Nol war, and the "new people" of the

[6]The U.S. dropped more bombs on the rural areas of Cambodia than were dropped on Germany in the whole of World War II.

towns on whom the *Khmers Rouges* mainly visited their atrocities for having caused all their ills.

The *Khmers Rouges* arrived in Phnom Penh—some reports have it—after the Vietnamese had first broken the perimeter for them. The towns were emptied, the genocide and destruction began. China suggested to Sihanouk that he return to Phnom Penh as Head of State of the Democratic Kampuchea his *Khmer Rouge* allies were creating without him. This took much courage: for the Prince already had glimmerings of what manner of tyranny the *Khmers Rouges* were running—and he wanted to soften it if he could. When a friend of the writer's, one of his close advisers, begged to go with him in the plane from Peking, the Prince refused saying, "They will kill you for sure, and they may well kill me".

So it was that Sihanouk became in his own words[7] a purely puppet Head of State, a prisoner in the Royal Palace. He was permitted contact with the outside world only through *Khmer Rouge* leader Khieu Samphan—of whom he writes, "There was no difficulty about recognizing the depth of (Khieu Samphan's) long-nurtured hatred for the monarchy and particularly for Sihanouk".[8] As is well known, the effect on a prisoner of having but one person to communicate through is to give that intermediary a disproportionate influence on the captive's mind. Khieu Samphan dominates *Prisonnier des Khmères Rouges* as, with a mixture of horror and fascination, he dominates Prince Sihanouk today. Through Khieu Samphan the Prince remains—in the words of a French diplomat who observed him at the August 1989 Paris Conference—"still prisoner of the *Khmers Rouges*".

Whether or not Khieu Samphan's influence amounted to "brain washing" properly speaking—and the evidence strongly suggests that it did—the Prince became and remains adamantly convinced of the immense power and virtual invincibility of the *Khmers Rouges*. By spreading this message, exaggerating both their political and military strength, he has helped the *Khmers Rouges* unwittingly but invaluably. For it became the Western line that the *Khmers Rouges* had to be given a share of power in any new regime in Cambodia (irrespective of the wishes of the Cambodians) or the country would dissolve into civil war. For Britain and France this was a relapse into the appeasement of the unappeasable that had led these countries to give the Sudentenland to Hitler in 1938 in defiance of the wishes of the Czechoslovak people.

[7]op. cit. p.89.
[8]op. cit. p.112.

In 1988, in evident emotional distress, Prince Sihanouk told the writer "I don't like the *Khmers Rouges*. I hate the *Khmers Rouges*. They killed 19 of my children and grandchildren. But they are so strong, so powerful that we have to deal with them". His entire book, *Prisonnier des Khmères Rouges* amounts to a dissertation on these few words. It sets out in detail the atrocities of the *Khmers Rouges* (see particularly the harrowing description on p.177), and how Sihanouk himself lived in daily fear of assassination. Yet it is at the same time an apologia for being obliged to yield to such odious mentors:

> After learning of the terrible misfortunes of my people . . . I had my head shaved . . . in 1977 as a sign of mourning and contrition, mourning for the holocaust of my people, the massacre of my children and grandchildren. An act of contrition for the support I gave to the Khmer Rouge . . . . [9]

This is the memoir of a perhaps over-sensitive man of exceptional charm, a lover of life and of culture, a Buddhist who strove to eschew hatred and violence, who was nevertheless plunged into the horror of the abyss. It shows how such trauma can destroy the will and the self-esteem of so firm-willed and confident a man as the Prince was when the writer first met him in 1956. In a brief forward to his book he summarizes his state of mind when he confesses "I had, and I have, no hope".

Sihanouk did not condemn the Vietnamese invasion. Like his countrymen he welcomed it, but regretted that it was Vietnam and not the world community that had intervened:

> Jimmy Carter told me in public that the Phnom Penh regime is "the worst violator of human rights in the world"—a few days later he caused me consternation . . . when he disapproved Senator McGovern's urgent call for a UN intervention force to liberate Cambodia from its executioners. The frontiers of Cambodia couldn't be violated even if a whole people is condemned to put up with a frightful tyranny . . . [10]

and:

> Our people were coming to the very pit of misery and misfortune. In the end I said to myself that when it comes down to it, it's perhaps high time

[9]op. cit. p.133.
[10]op. cit. p.203.

that a foreign country, even Vietnam, should intervene to put an end to this intolerable situation. And I ask myself today if it makes sense to reproach honourable personalities . . . for collaborating with the Vietnamese.[11]

China plucked Sihanouk out of Cambodia by air as the Vietnamese forces advanced on Phnom Penh in January 1979. Under pressure from China he went to the United Nations to put the *Khmer Rouge* case against Vietnam for its invasion. Dramatically he decided "to liberate myself from the intolerable control of *Angkar*". Secretly he passed a note to Andrew Young, then US Permanent Representative to the United Nations. At 2 a.m. that night he and Princess Monique were led out of the Waldorf Astoria Hotel by agents of the FBI while his *Khmer Rouge* minders slept.

But Prince Sihanouk was not to escape the *Khmers Rouges* so easily. For it was not long before the United States and China jointly put pressure—directly and through ASEAN—on the Prince to serve again as Head of Democratic Kampuchea. The Prince explains what happened in an extraordinarily revealing passage. It demonstrates his new pliancy and his disgust with himself for becoming once again a mere tool of his ghastly adversaries:

Peking insisted that I should ally myself with the *Khmers Rouges* who . . . meant to install a communist regime, defender of the Chinese marches. Powerless and isolated before so many interconnecting pressures I abdicated and agreed to enter the tripartite coalition of Democratic Kampuchea. At the insistence of ASEAN . . . I signed at Kuala Lumpur on 22 June 1982 an agreement to form the "Coalition Government of Democratic Kampuchea" whose essential task would be to conduct the struggle to "liberate Cambodia" . . . As for me, with death in my soul, I found myself once again Head and President of the most terrible enemies who had massacred or caused to die two million Cambodians—among them thirty members of my own family . . . An ignominious union . . . [12]

This key passage also reveals *realpolitik* as played by the democracies in the eighties. Briefly, Adolf Hitler had revealed, with particular starkness, the recurrent emergence throughout history of the dark underside of humanity in the mass. And the civilized world had set up the United Nations with the primary aim of preventing further repetition of such horrors as the Nazis had perpetrated. But Stalin, who had perpetrated and was still perpetrating

[11]op. cit. p.312.
[12]op. cit. p.402. For clarity in translation the passage is rendered in the first person throughout.

slaughters on a vast scale himself, was simultaneously arousing such fears in the democracies that they came to believe that they too, were obliged to countenance atrocities to prevent the spread of communism. The argument seemed overwhelming: was it not obvious that another Belsen was a small price to pay to prevent nuclear war?

The logical result of such thinking was the United States' decision to join with China in backing the *Khmers Rouges* to fight to restore their despotism against the manifest will of the Cambodian people. For China and the US the purpose was not simply to persuade Vietnam to evacuate Cambodia—as we have seen there were other, more effective ways of doing that—but to undermine the Vietnamese communists who had defeated them both in battle: a *Khmer Rouge* restoration in Cambodia would menace Vietnam itself, and possibly aid in its destabilization. The Sino-American aim was, as the saying goes, "to bleed Vietnam on the battlefield of Cambodia".

This was no lone US decision with China, since Britain and France—the other two permanent Western members of the Security Council—by and large went along with this. So did the six ASEAN countries, all of whom claim to be considered democracies. Prince Sihanouk has been much reviled for playing the *Khmers Rouges's* game. But the Prince is only one man whose harrowing experiences would have equally enfeebled many another. Any criticism should more justly be applied to those Western countries who bent the Prince to their purpose.

But before making such criticism, the eternal problem of *realpolitik* must be considered. Just how far are national states above all moral considerations? Is the self-preservation of the nation-state justification for *any* iniquity? Maybe that is inevitably so. But it is more dubious that *all* moral considerations should be ignored in forwarding the further flung and less vital policies of sovereign states. For it may be argued that in embracing atrocity, a nation is destroying the very values it represents and which are at once the essential reason and the justification for its self-preservation. And it has been argued that the brutalization of foreign policy is a cause of the kind of social malaises (crime, drugs, racism, alienation and so forth) that are ravaging the United States and the Soviet Union, and threaten to engulf Europe too.

Cambodia is but a small country, but its history since 1968 demands wider attention. For it suggests that the time has come for informed opinion to reconsider the value-destructive aspects of *realpolitik* with a view to bringing to an end a period in history where the very word "immoral" lies unused, and even unusable, in those departments of states which deal with foreign matters.

THE PHNOM PENH GOVERNMENT

As has been mentioned, the Phnom Penh government's period of tutelage by the Vietnamese was prolonged by the scarcity of educated people after Pol Pot's massacres, and by the lack of resources to reconstruct after the near total destruction of everything—not just infrastructure and factories but the very irrigation systems that enabled rice to be grown. The East Europeans and the Soviet Union did send considerable aid. As a result, when the UN 14-nation military reconnaissance team reported on their visit to Cambodia in early August 1989 they deplored the lack of almost all resources and advised that any UN mission would not only have to bring in all it needed from abroad but would have to repair elements of infrastructure—such as roads—themselves (cf. the first six pages or so to have been released of the mission's more than 200 page report).

Even as late as 1986 Vietnamese advisers were much in evidence and the country had the dreary, repressive air of Vietnam itself. It was in that year that Vietnam announced that its forces would leave Cambodia variously "by", "in", or "at the end of" 1990. From then on Vietnamese and Cambodians put their minds to building up a sufficiently strong and autonomous Cambodia to have some chance of survival after this withdrawal. In January 1987 the writer found that Prime Minister Hun Sen alone spoke to him in straight, concise, pragmatic terms. The other ministers he met still wasted time with communist jargon. Two years later, in February 1989, no one at all, not even junior officials in the provinces spoke in those dated ideological terms.

An immense change had taken place in those two years: Cambodia had rediscovered its personality—for good and for bad (the old corruption that dogged Sihanouk and helped destroy Lon Nol is rearing its head again—party purity is on the way out). The Cambodian army, which looked like a rabble in 1987, had some efficient-looking units by 1989. And the rural population which had simply sat back and let the Vietnamese get on with things, was taking its responsibilities for self-defence very seriously indeed by 1989. Throughout the populous areas of the country the *Sena Chun* (Home Guard) is on the alert night and day: perhaps a hundred thousand strong with a motley collection of weapons. However rag-tag a force, the *Sena Chun* achieves two things—it expresses morale, the determination to die rather than let the *Khmers Rouges* return, and it preserves the country from the beginning of the end in guerrilla war, when the government abandons the countryside each night to the guerrillas. That—in the opinion of the writer who observed its consequences—was perhaps the main factor that ensured the eventual defeat of South Vietnam.

We have already noted that Vietnam, as a necessary corollary to its military withdrawal, acquiesced in the Cambodian government entering into negotiations with Prince Sihanouk with a view to the Prince's return as Head of State even though the deal would mean Cambodia leaving the "socialist" group of nations. From December 1979 to July 1989 Premier Hun Sen and Prince Sihanouk met half a dozen times and in between meetings continued negotiations through their chief advisers. One Cambodian negotiator told the writer early in this series of contacts that the Cambodian government was fully aware that the Prince had suffered severely psychologically as a result of his *Khmer Rouge* experiences. But so had so many others in Cambodia: "the *Khmer Rouge* trauma"—as the Prince calls it—was something Cambodians often had to overcome in dealings with each other. The government therefore appreciated the need for patience and understanding in its dealings with the Prince. But it had to be recognized that the Prince might be so far under *Khmer Rouge* control that he would be unable to make the deal with Phnom Penh that he obviously wanted, because that would of necessity involve breaking with the *Khmers Rouges*.

The Cambodian government therefore began to pursue a parallel policy—rapprochement with Thailand. The writer asked Prime Minister Hun Sen about this. The Premier replied that the "cleanest", swiftest, least bloody solution of the Cambodian problem was a deal with Prince Sihanouk. For the world considered Sihanouk represented Cambodian legitimacy. The return of Sihanouk and internationally-supervised elections would guarantee universal diplomatic recognition, the UN Seat in the General Assembly, and UN and bilateral aid. As another minister put it, "The Prince would return with the key to the World Bank in his pocket". But if the Prince could not break free from the *Khmers Rouges* and their Chinese backers, then peace could be built less "cleanly", less quickly, with more blood spilt—but in the long run just as effectively—on the foundation of *rapprochement* with Thailand.

Hun Sen reminded the writer that he had always stressed that any Cambodian government must have the best possible relations with Bangkok as much as with Hanoi. Relations with Bangkok had been ruined by the *Khmers Rouges*. When they were in power they had alienated Thailand, and when they fled from the Vietnamese advance they had established themselves on Thai territory, making Thailand their ally against Vietnam, so ensuring bad relations between Thailand and his government. But, with the Vietnamese withdrawal, the Thais had every reason to want a stable Cambodia and the suppression of the heavily armed *Khmers Rouges* straddling the frontier. As for Cambodia, the re-opening of the frontier, the re-establishment of communications (road, rail, air, and telecom) would at a stroke end the isolation of Cambodia imposed by the Sino-Western blockade, and begin the isolation of the *Khmers Rouges*. This would open up trade, investment, and a more normal existence—much improving morale. And militarily, an open frontier would tip the strategic balance firmly in favour of the defenders of Cambodia. Another minister made the point that success with Thailand would encourage the Prince to do a deal—first because he could not abide being left out of a solution, and second because it would lessen his fears: for once Thailand had acted to isolate them, the danger of the *Khmers Rouges* returning would be virtually nil.

THE PARIS CONFERENCE, JULY/AUGUST 1989

With this résumé of history behind us, we can now look briefly at the position in mid-1989, just before Prince Sihanouk and Premier Hun Sen met on July 24, which was to be followed the next week by the opening of the Paris Conference on Cambodia called by Co-Chairs France and Indonesia.

The prospects for the Conference were brighter than had been expected a few weeks earlier when the French had first mooted the idea.

First, as we have seen, Hun Sen and Sihanouk had a deal but for a decision due to be taken by them on July 24 on what exactly they should offer the *Khmers Rouges* by way of participation in a supra-governmental authority for the arranging and holding of internationally-supervised free elections. As both sides recognized that there could be no return for this purpose of armed *Khmer Rouge* cadres there appeared to be no overriding impediment to coming to terms on this matter.

Second, fears that China might prove irrational and aggressive after the Tienanmen shootings, had been allayed with at least two major non-communist powers being assured by Beijing that it intended to stick to Li Peng's earlier assurance that once Vietnamese troops had been proved to have left Cambodia, China would cease arming the *Khmers Rouges*. To some extent, China's policy towards the Cambodian problem was in part dictated by its unwillingness to be isolated as the sole supporter of the *Khmers Rouges* at a time when it was anxious to rebuild bridges following the "Tienanmen massacre", especially with the South-East Asians.

Third, President Bush, immediately after his election in November 1988, had asked for a review of US policy towards Indochina and Cambodia in particular. As a result, by April 1989 the Americans had obtained and collated an adequate body of information on Cambodia for the first time in 15 years. They understood at last that the Cambodian government was no longer a puppet of the Vietnamese but had become the least communist of communist governments and had gone a long way towards "devietnamizing" itself. They knew the thinking of Hun Sen and his team of advisers. They knew the general line if not the details of the deal he and Prince Sihanouk had all but concluded. They appreciated that if Sihanouk kept his part of the bargain and broke with the *Khmers Rouges*, then Hun Sen would be bound to keep his part of the bargain and hold genuine free elections, thereby—if the people so willed—irreversibly ending Cambodia's membership of the "socialist bloc". They also appreciated that the Vietnamese almost certainly intended to go, and not to cheat by leaving behind part of their army in Cambodian uniform. Finally, the Americans knew from a number of sources, including ex-Lon Nol General In Tam, who had just visited Cambodia, that the Vietnamese had not colonized Cambodia as Chinese, Sihanoukian and *Khmer Rouge* propaganda had it: that there were certainly not "a million Vietnamese colonists" in Cambodia and that it was dubious if the number of largely indigenous Vietnamese in Cambodia even reached the figure of Vietnamese residents in Sihanouk's time.

After he had seen the new Cambodian dossier in May prior to meeting NATO heads of government, President Bush was understood to have said that he wished to have nothing to do with the *Khmers Rouges*: that they should be marginalized. The Americans said that they were no longer insisting on "quadripartitism"—that is, Prince Sihanouk's plan that all four Cambodian parties—the Phnom Penh Government, the Sihanoukists, the *Khmers Rouges*, and Sonn Sann's KPNLF—should each have a quarter share of power in an interim government prior to elections. The British government, always a mirror of American policy over Cambodia, shifted its attitude within a day or two of the State Department. Because the one thing–as we have seen–that the Phnom Penh government could not accept is any return of the *Khmers Rouges*, this apparent decision no longer to demand that seemed to open the way to a successful conference—especially given China's position and the state of negotiations between Prince and Premier.

Few were surprised when the Prince arrived from China to meet Hun Sen on July 24 and failed to conclude the deal. The French pointed out that the vacillating Prince always took a few days to shed the attitudes he adopted when in China. Conference goers explained this as Sihanouk simply being canny enough not to play his trump card too early: the Prince, they said, would produce his *coup de théâtre* when the foreign ministers reassembled to close the Conference. Those who knew the Prince's anguished state of mind—including his closest advisers—were worried that the Prince would not—with his old virtuosity—leap in the Conference circus from the *Khmer Rouge* horse onto the approaching Hun Sen horse. They knew only that intellectually the Prince remained convinced that the Vietnamese departure provided him with his last opportunity to break with the *Khmers Rouges*—and so at once put himself right with his conscience, with the Cambodian people whom he had tried so hard and so unsuccessfully to save from terrible tribulation, and with history as the last of the Norodoms and the last too, of an immemorial line of kings.

So long as Vietnam remained in Cambodia, Sihanouk had the respectable enough excuse that the higher interest of the nation demanded that he work even with its worst enemies to oust it. His closest friends knew that, at 67, the Prince had soon to escape the thrall of Khieu Samphan if he were to return home to the acclaim of government, people, and the world to assume the Presidency. Only by making that break could he die, finally justified, in the neutral non-communist Cambodian buffer-state for which, as a youthful king, he had achieved independence, and which, as a young man, he had built up to be one of the most prosperous, happy and beautiful countries in Asia. They knew too, though, that his wife, Princess Monique, and his son, Prince Ranaridh, did not want to return to Phnom Penh, but were content to build up—for Ranaridh at least—a lucrative army with US weapons—and that these family pressures weighed on the Prince emotionally. They knew also that Chhorn Hay, one of the Prince's jailers in Phnom Penh, still had access to his entourage and that the Prince and Princess believe that the *Khmers Rouges* could assassinate them "even in the Royal Palace". They knew that the Prince was rarely out of sight of some *Khmer Rouge* cadre during his entire time in Paris—and they knew the effect of this surveillance on his tormented mind. In a word, those closest to Sihanouk knew that unless the United States came out unequivocally against the *Khmers Rouges* and utterly refused to back him further if he remained with allies so odious to any democrat, then the Prince would all but certainly renege on his understanding with Hun Sen. The Prince's advisers therefore despatched at least one neutral emissary to bring to Assistant Secretary Solomon's notice that only the strongest possible American stand against the *Khmers Rouges* could effect a break between the Prince and the *Khmers Rouges*.

In the event Secretary of State Baker scuppered the Conference from the start with his opening speech. His exact words (speech July 30, 1989) were:

> The United States strongly believes that the *Khmers Rouges* should play no role in Cambodia's future. We are prepared however, to support Prince Sihanouk should he deem it necessary to accept the inclusion of all Khmer factions in an interim coalition or an interim authority.

It will be seen from what has gone before, that had the Secretary of State stopped after that first sentence, the Conference would have had every chance of success. First, the message would have reached all 18 nations present that the US would not accept *Khmer Rouge* participation in government prior to consultation of the Cambodian people. Most of the ASEAN countries, plus France, Britain, Canada, Australia and Japan would have backed the US line. Prince Ranaridh would have appreciated that there was no future for his father's small army of which he was Commander-in-Chief because it would receive no weapons from the US unless his father broke with the *Khmers Rouges*.

In these circumstances Ranaridh might have urged his father to accept American backing to get the best possible deal with Phnom Penh. Above all, China would have found itself all but isolated—as it had half expected—and forced to stick to its promise to cease arming the *Khmers Rouges* after verification of the Vietnamese departure. France and Indonesia, the Conference Co-Chairs, would have been deeply grateful for the breakthrough. Prime Minister Chatichai of Thailand would have been exceedingly relieved that his *rapprochement* with Hun Sen was now acceptable to the US and, albeit grudgingly, to China. Cambodia and Vietnam would undoubtedly have agreed immediately to accept UN verification of the Vietnamese withdrawal—which idea had been obnoxious to them given *Khmer Rouge* presence in the General Assembly. And even if the Prince had still baulked at returning to Phnom Penh as Head of State, peace could have come quickly via the Thai alternative.

That second sentence of Mr. Baker's was thus the precipitating cause, both of the failure of the Conference, and of the appeal to arms that followed it. Not one of the countries present did anything to stop the drift to war: but then what country can readily withstand the pressures of two superpowers on the same issue at the same time? The Fourth Indochina War—a proxy war between the *Khmers Rouges*, Sihanouk and Sonn Sann on the one hand, and the defenders of Cambodia from the evils of the *Khmers Rouges* on the other—broke out in late September during the last stages of the Vietnamese withdrawal. It began with a *Khmer Rouge* assault on the strategic position of what was once the gem mining village of Pailin. The loss of Pailin would put Battambang, the second city in Cambodia, in the front line. Much more *Khmer Rouge* activity throughout Cambodia must be expected. As Premier Hun Sen said when asked what he thought as he left the Conference: "Many people will die unnecessarily".

As the United States was adequately informed as a result of the policy review, and as it knew that the Cambodian people were overwhelmingly against any return whatever of the *Khmers Rouges* and that no Cambodian government could negotiate the return of any of them with arms, and as the United States must have been aware of China's position, it is all but impossible that Mr. Baker did not know when he spoke the fatal sentence that he was torpedoing the Conference before it even got under way. Cambodia specialists saw through the American attempt to blame Hanoi and Phnom Penh for the failure of the Conference because of their "intransigance" in not accepting *Khmer Rouge* participation in government. The State Department suggested off the record that the new Bush Administration "had not yet gotten its act together" over Cambodia and Afghanistan. Given the size of the US governmental machine this might just be the case. But one fact strongly suggests that US policy approves the trial of force now in progress, and that therefore the US Administration is abetting the return of the *Khmers Rouges* to Cambodia knowing that this will menace Vietnam and the Soviet bases there. This is why during the Conference the Administration sought and obtained Congressional permission to send lethal weapons to Sihanouk. This was of little importance in itself. But the political message was clear. Had the provision of weapons been made conditional upon the Prince forswearing the *Khmers Rouges*, the Prince would have understood that if he remained with them, he would forfeit essential American support. As it was, the provision of arms without condition gave the Prince the overwhelming message that the fickle Americans would not once again help him escape his jailers: they wanted him to remain with them still.

The prospect of a Fourth Indochina War is already causing some of America's European allies—who have little interest in Cambodia for itself—to fear a rift in NATO. On the one hand the Americans appear to be exploiting communist internal difficulties in Vietnam and the Soviet Union by "pouring gasoline on the dying embers of 45 years of Indochina wars", as one diplomat put it. On the other hand, the continental Europeans want to douse the flames of regional conflict in order to lower the level of East–West confrontation for fear of provoking the hardliners into dropping the Iron Curtain again and returning to neo-Stalinism. Given the situation between the two Germanies alone, attempts at destabilization of Vietnam could have unforeseeable effects. From a European point of view there is no need for such a policy apart from pure revenge. For Cambodia, even now, could be brought peacefully out from the socialist bloc. As for Vietnam, as the Europeans see things, it is after all leaving Cambodia precisely in order to get enmeshed in trade and aid from the capitalist world. The Europeans profess to see some signs that evolution could take place if Vietnam were but to take its place again among the South East Asian nations.

THE PROSPECT OF WAR

The outcome of the war cannot be foreseen. At a press conference during the Paris talks, Premier Hun Sen gave his estimate of the strength of the *Khmers*

Rouges as 14,000–15,000. This is far lower than Prince Sihanouk's figures which have been as high as 60,000. Hun Sen's estimate though is consistent with the demographic evidence. According to Thai and UN sources, there are some 50,000 people in *Khmer Rouge* camps and up to 30,000 more in the so called "secret" camps, making a total population under *Khmer Rouge* control of 80,000 or thereabouts. Assuming that a maximum of one-in-four of the total population is of any appreciable military value, one arrives at a maximum strength of 20,000. The actual figure is almost certainly less than this—so Hun Sen's total of 14,000–15,000 would seem to fit the population figures.

So long as the *Khmers Rouges* are encamped on the Thai border, denied access to the populated areas, and compelled to carry all their equipment and food over mountain and through jungle and brousse, much of their strength must be allocated to securing lines of communication, and to guarding their camps to prevent mass defections (500 families are reported to have broken out shortly before the Paris Conference). A French expert on the *Khmers Rouges* stated in 1988 that they could only sustain 5,000 to 8,000 men in the field within Cambodia at any one time, the higher figure being in the dry season. At the end of 1988, the writer was told (by one of the ministers responsible) that the Cambodian army had captured important *Khmer Rouge* documents which detailed the strength of the various divisions. Only two of these contained over 500 men, and some of the others were of negligible strength. The total came to under 10,000.

From these figures—which come within the very broad gap between the upper and lower estimates of Western intelligence which for once cannot rely on either satellite or "sigint"—one can reasonably conclude that so long as the Cambodian army can contain the *Khmers Rouges* on the frontier and not let their main force regroup in populated areas, then their menace is containable. Although they would pose a considerable threat to an untried army and an ill-equipped Home Guard, a *Khmer Rouge* victory is by no means a foregone conclusion. Nor is it certain that the war will endanger any provincial capital, or spread so much that the present steady, indeed accelerating, reconstruction of the country is slowed. Much will depend on the Cambodian troops showing a will to fight, and on the *Khmer Rouge* morale being as low as some reports from Western observers as well as from Phnom Penh suggest.

But any victory of the *Khmers Rouges*—even the taking of Pailin, let alone say the temporary occupation of part of Battambang—would be likely to have a disproportionate effect on the country's new, but very brittle, morale. Terror of the *Khmers Rouges* spreads right across the country to the Vietnamese frontier—and beyond. In addition, a breakthrough to the populated areas would, as we have seen, increase *Khmer Rouge* effectives sustainable within Cambodia by a good 5,000 men straight away. The *Khmers Rouges* could then live off the country and forcibly recruit. The Home Guard, which can and does effectively see off small bands of guerrillas, could not handle such a threat—it would collapse.

Should the guerrillas prove so successful, the question then is—what would Vietnam do faced with a *Khmer Rouge* threat to its own borders? Premier Hun Sen has said that he reserves the right to call on the Vietnamese to assist Cambodia once again. And the Vietnamese have not ruled out a return. But it is quite clear that this is no part of their plan and that they would only return with the greatest reluctance. Perhaps they would merely straighten the frontier to remove such dangerous anomalies as the "Parrot's Beak". But some military experts say that the only logical defence line is the east bank of the broad Mekong river—on the western side of which lies Phnom Penh. Would the Thais advance to the West bank and partition Cambodia? Could a Thai–Vietnamese war begin, perhaps by accident? This is speculation—but it serves to show that renewed war in Cambodia is a regional problem, most unlikely to be confined merely to Cambodia itself.

The Vietnamese have said that when they leave, they leave with no intention of returning—and that the *Khmers Rouges* will then become a problem for those states that rearmed them or connived at their resurgence—China, the USA, Britain, Thailand, and the other ASEAN countries. And indeed, were TV crews to send back searing images of a *Khmer Rouge* return, the West—even the USA—might be forced to take some more decisive action. In which case the Vietnamese gamble to implicate the West could yet come off.

SCENARIOS

To answer the remaining questions asked at the beginning of this chapter—can the war be stopped, or at least can the circumstances in which it is fought be improved to give the people of Cambodia a better chance of fighting off their attackers?—we must consider likely scenarios in the light of the story we set out above:

Scenario I: The *Khmers Rouges* want as quick a war as possible, and as decisive a victory as can be achieved in the few months before international sentiment again builds up to demand a further JIM meeting in Jakarta, or the promised resumption of the 18-nation Conference—if not in Paris, perhaps in Asia. It is possible that, because Cambodian morale is so brittle, a relatively small victory could lead to collapse. But short of this, it is unlikely that the *Khmers Rouges* will be able to overrun the country in the short term—even aided, when they look like gaining ground, by the smaller but still significant forces of Prince Sihanouk and Son Sann: aid which would complicate the clear-cut issue of resisting Pol Pot both for the outside world and for many Cambodians. However there is a substantial chance that they will be able to advance to the populated areas and begin to establish themselves, so giving them a springboard for a final advance by the time the nations reconsider Cambodia's fate. This is probably what the United States and China hope for—that would greatly strengthen the *Khmers Rouges* in their demand for a major share in government. If they got it, the government would all but certainly collapse, and even if it did not the *Khmers Rouges* would be poised to take state power with the captive Sihanouk still their unwilling stooge.

Doubtless many states would recognize such a government cloaked by Sihanouk, and the Cambodian problem would be "resolved" only to pose itself once again when the *Khmers Rouges* tire of Sihanouk. Whether or not, and at what stage, the Vietnamese would react, either by straightening the frontier, or by outright partition on the Mekong line, cannot be foreseen. A second major Vietnamese intervention cannot be ruled out. In any of these cases the attitude of Thailand might well be sympathetic to some limited Vietnamese involvement, with Thailand perhaps recovering its "lost provinces"—Battambang for example—in Western Cambodia. Now that the two countries have regular diplomatic contact at foreign minister level the risks of a Thai–Vietnam clash might be minimized.

On the other hand, events might by then be so out of control that a Thai–Vietnam war would break out in any case. In any of these circumstances it is all but certain that moderates—the practitioners of *glasnost* and *perestroika* in Vietnam and the Soviet Union, would be hard put to maintain their policy of accommodation with the West. The tenuous *détentes* between the USA and the USSR, and the USSR and China would be at risk. The world situation could alter for the worse, especially if some similar American bellicosity occurred in Afghanistan or some other conflict region. That is the worst case scenario—a scenario in which the West as a whole and the USA in particular would have to share the blame equally with China. The effect of public opinion on Western governments supporting the Sino-American line could be grave for the Alliance. For human rights are taken increasingly seriously in many democracies despite the lip service commonly afforded them by governments. Already more than half the German people—according to the polls—consider the United States more of a threat to world peace than the Soviet Union. This could well become the general perception in Western Europe if events in Cambodia and Afghanistan continue on their present course. That would bode ill for the NATO Alliance.

Scenario II: The previous scenario predicated no action by Thailand to stop the drift to all-out war. It assumed that Premier Chatichai's government, like other governments around the world, will find itself unable to resist the combined displeasure of China and America. But there is a more hopeful view. Far from accepting a Sino-American *fait accompli*, Chatichai was already acting vigorously to prevent war at the time of writing in October 1989. He let it be known soon after the failure in Paris that he wished to recover the spirit of JIM which linked the withdrawal of Vietnamese forces with a cessation of arms supplies to the three resistance factions. He made clear his views to Sihanouk, Son San and the *Khmers Rouges*, remarking that so far as Thailand is concerned the 300,000-odd Cambodian "displaced persons" on Thai soil have now become an internal problem of Cambodia's and should not be armed. Chatichai invited Premier Hun Sen to Bangkok—giving him the opportunity to demonstrate the improved security around parts of the border area by walking across the footbridge beside the blocked road and railway into Thailand. At the same time, Chatichai's colleagues were reportedly saying privately that Thailand would welcome recognition of the Phnom Penh government by any nation that felt it would extend it.

Chatichai needs international encouragement for pursuing a course of action which some Nobel laureates are suggesting should merit him the Nobel Peace Prize.

If Thailand gets international support, then the "peace through Thailand" solution already discussed could become reality. And there is even a chance—slight though it is because of the psychological trauma the Prince has suffered—of Sihanouk finally screwing himself up to exchange the bloodied cap of the Head of *Khmer Rouge*-dominated Democratic Kampuchea, for the more honourable hat of Head of State of a non-communist, truly democratic Cambodia. Deprived of the prestige of their UN seat, and widespread international recognition, the *Khmers Rouges* would revert to being a band of vicious murderers in the brousse, jungle and mountains of Cambodia. With no more arms coming from China and faced with universal opposition within and without Cambodia, they would wither before too long as discipline broke down and defections mounted.

If Thailand gets the support Chatichai deserves from the West, then pressure on President Bush's Administration—already mounting in Congress—could become irresistible. There would be no need to lose face. All the Administration would have to do would be (i) to withdraw that fateful second sentence in

Secretary of State Baker's policy speech of July 30 to the Paris Conference; and (ii) announce that, in the now changed circumstances, the USA could no longer support the Prince's position on *Khmer Rouge* participation in government prior to a referendum or elections. China would then be faced with isolation and with having to modify its policies in accordance with its intentions announced in November 1988: the *Khmers Rouges* would then receive no more arms. But China, like America, would lose no face—for China could declare that it had consistently supported Prince Sihanouk since the 1950s, and was now happy to see the outcome it had always striven for: his return to a neutral Cambodia as Head of State.

There are of course other scenarios which are variations on these two. But enough has been said to show that—with a modicum of goodwill and common sense, history need not always end in tragedy: the second scenario is possible if the non-communist countries concerned with the problem can find the courage *together* to stand up to China and the United States. And it is much easier to do this knowing that both these superpowers have an acceptable fall back position, and that neither has any overriding need to destabilize the Indochinese peninsula.

A young engineer bears evidence of the importance of foreign aid
(Pete Brabban/Oxfam)

Calm waters ahead for Cambodia? *(Jill Arace/Oxfam)*

REFERENCE SECTION

CAMBODIA OR KAMPUCHEA?

The names Cambodia and Kampuchea are both transliterations of the country's traditional name in the Khmer language, which is sometimes rendered phonetically as "Kambuja". Cambodia was adopted as the English spelling for the French transliteration *Cambodge*. In this book the name Cambodia is used as a general historical term and the name Kampuchea when emphasizing proper titles (e.g. Democratic Kampuchea).

Under Sihanouk the country was known in the West as the Kingdom of Cambodia. However, under Lon Nol's Khmer Republic (1970–75) official use of the transliteration Cambodia (but not Kampuchea) was apparently discouraged because of its colonial connotations. The Pol Pot regime (1975–79) changed the country's title to Democratic Cambodia or Democratic Kampuchea and it was at this time that "Kampuchea" began to appear as the country's name in the Western media. After Pol Pot's overthrow, the new regime adopted the title of People's Republic of Kampuchea. When it was announced in April 1989 that the country was to be called the State of Cambodia, most Western newspapers claimed that "Kampuchea" had reverted to "Cambodia", although in fact equal emphasis should have been placed on the PRK government's dropping of the designation "People's Republic" as a concession to Prince Sihanouk and the West.

POPULATION

Due to the social and economic disruption caused by nearly 20 years of war, reliable statistics on Cambodia are hard to come by. Total population in 1989 was estimated as over 7,500,000 in Cambodia itself, of whom around 750,000 live in the capital, Phnom Penh. The country's second city is Battambang. Kompong Som is the principal port.

In addition, approximately 330,000 Cambodians are living in and around refugee camps on the Thai side of the border. Of these, some 260,000 are resident in the eight principal "civilian camps", under the effective control of the *Khmers Rouges* (Site 8, Bo Rai, Ta Luan, Natrao, Huay Chan), the KPNLF (Site 2, Sol Sann) and the ANS (Green Hill). Satellite military camps outside the main sites contain an estimated 60,000 CGDK soldiers (the majority being *Khmers Rouges*) and a further 10,000 civilians. By far the largest of the camps is Site 2, which with a population of over 150,000 is the second most heavily populated Cambodian city.

Between 1975 and 1986, over 200,000 Cambodian refugees left Thailand for other countries, principally the USA (136,000) and France (32,000).

ECONOMIC ACTIVITY

Cambodia remains an overwhelmingly agricultural country, with over 90 per cent of the populace dependent on it for a living. Some small-scale industry is gradually being reintroduced after the virtual collapse of the country's economy during the late '70s. The family remains the basic economic unit, with groups of 10–15 families organized together as a *krom samaki* ("solidarity group"), working individual or communal paddy land by sharing their labour, farm implements and animals.

Rice is the principal crop and staple food; other agricultural products include fruit and vegetables, beans, natural rubber, spices (notably sesame and black pepper), sugar-cane and sugar-palm juice, pigs, poultry and cattle. There is a limited timber industry. The potentially rich fishing sector remains underdeveloped.

The vast majority of Cambodia's exports, (which include rice, rubber, timber, tobacco and fish) go to Vietnam and to Socialist-bloc countries.

Refugees on the Thai side of the border are largely dependent on international and non-governmental organization (NGO) assistance co-ordinated by the United Nations Border Relief Operation (UNBRO).

COMPARATIVE DEVELOPMENT INDICATORS

	Cambodia	*Laos*	*Vietnam*	*Thailand*
General:				
Total population 1979 (millions)	7.7	3.8	62.8	53.3
Life expectancy (yrs)	49	49	62	66
Crude birth rate	42	42	32	23
Crude death rate	17	17	10	7
Under-fives death rate (1987)	208	163	91	51
Infant mortality rate (1987)	133	111	65	40

Health and nutrition:

	Cambodia	Laos	Vietnam	Thailand
% of children with mild:moderate/ severe malnutrition (1986)	17:3	n.a.	40:10	27:0
% of children immunized (1986–7)	37.0	28.0	51.0	80.0
% of population with access to health services	50.0	n.a.	80.0	70.0
% of population with access to drinking water	3.0	21.0	41.0	66.0

FOREIGN AID

In addition to receiving bilateral economic assistance from Vietnam and the socialist countries (estimated at $100 million per year), the State of Cambodia plays host to around 30 Western NGOs, which provide about $10,000,000 per year in relief and development assistance.

Due to its refusal to recognize the Phnom Penh government, UN assistance within Cambodia is largely restricted to emergency aid. Most Western governments, with the exception of Australia, offer little in the way of bilateral aid to the State of Cambodia itself. UN agencies and Western governments do, however, offer considerable support to the refugee community on the Thai border. During the period 1982–86, funds committed to UNICEF-assisted projects within Cambodia totalled approximately $16,500,000 in the same period, cash contributions to UNBRO, targeted at the refugees on the Thai frontier, amounted to around $79,000,000.[1]

POLITICAL STRUCTURE

(1) STATE OF CAMBODIA

Constitution

Under its 1981 constitution (amended in 1989) the State of Cambodia is an independent sovereign state "moving step-by-step towards socialism", which acknowledges Buddhism as the state religion.

---

[1]Economic information presented here comes from a variety of sources, including the UN, FAO, and Oxfam (as presented in *Punishing the Poor*, by Eva Mysliwiec—Oxfam, 1988), and *Humanitarian Assistance in Kampuchea, (1989)*.

Legislative power in the State of Cambodia is vested in the 117-member National Assembly, which according to the constitution should be elected every five years by universal adult suffrage. At the time of writing, elections were due to be held in November 1989, the previous poll having taken place in 1981. The Assembly meets twice per year, and elects a Council of State from among its members as its permanent body.

Executive power is vested in a Council of Ministers (Cabinet), elected by the Assembly and responsible to it. In practice, effective political power rests with the ruling (and sole legal) party, the Cambodian People's Revolutionary Party.

THE DECREASE IN HUMANITARIAN ASSISTANCE
FROM THE UN AGENCIES

	1979-1981	*1981*
Agencies included ICRC, UNICEF, UNHCR, WFP, FAO	366.7 million	110.0 million

Government Contributions in Kind to UN Assisted Programmes (in 000s USD)

1982	1983	1984	1985	1986	1987
11,078	7,220	7,606	4,917	4,703	3,519

RECENT EMERGENCY AND DEVELOPMENT AID BUDGETS
(EXPRESSED AS AVERAGE US$ EXPENDITURE PER AGENCY)

	1987	*1988*	*1989*
Non-governmental agencies (total = 23)	$546,545	$740,538	$868,179
United Nations agencies (total = 3)	$5.25	$5.5	$6.0

GOVERNMENT AND PARTY LEADERSHIPS

Head of state: Heng Samrin, President of the Council of State

Members of the Council of Ministers

Hun Sen	Chairman; Foreign Affairs
Bou Thang	Vice-Chairman
Say Phouthang	Vice-Chairman; Chairman of Central Control Commission
Chea Soth	Vice-Chairperson
Kong Samol	Vice-Chairperson; Minister in charge of the Cabinet of the Council of Ministers
Say Chhum	Vice-Chairperson; Agriculture
Tea Banh	Vice-Chairperson; National Defence
Pung Peng Cheng	Minister-assistant to the Chairman of the Council of Ministers
Kong Korm	State Affairs Inspectorate
Koy Buntha	Social Affairs and War Invalids
Chea Chanto	Planning
Mrs Ho Hon	Industry
Sin Song	Interior
Chhay Than	Finance
Pen Navuth	Education
Ung Phan	Communications, Transport and Posts
Chheng Phon	Information, Press and Culture
Taing Sarim	Trade
Ouk Bun Chhoeun	Justice
Yith Kim Seng	Health
Khun Chhy	Minister attached to the Council of Ministers
Hor Nam Hong	Minister Assistant in charge of monitoring Foreign and Judicial Affairs
Cha Rieng	Chairman of the National Bank
(vacant)	Director General of General Directorate for Tourism
Sim Ka	Chairman of State Control Committee
Sam Sarit	Director of General Department for Rubber Plantations

Cambodian People's Revolutionary Party
General secretary: Heng Samrin.

Members of the political bureau: Heng Samrin, Chea Sim, Hun Sen, Say Phouthang, Bou Thang, Chea Soth, Ms Men Sam An, Math Ly, Nguon Nhel, Sar Kheng, Say Chhum, Tea Banh.

Alternate members: Chan Seng, Sin Song, Pol Saroeun, Sim Ka.

Members of the secretariat: Heng Samrin, Hun Sen, Bou Thang, Ms Men Sam An, Nay Pena, Sar Kheng, Say Chhum, Say Phouthang.

(2) COALITION GOVERNMENT OF DEMOCRATIC KAMPUCHEA

Democratic Kampuchea was the title of the *Khmer Rouge* regime which governed Cambodia from 1975–79, when it was replaced by the People's Republic of Kampuchea following the ousting of the *Khmers Rouges* by the Vietnamese Army and opposition guerrillas. It continued to be accorded official recognition by the overwhelming majority of United Nations member states, despite the fact that it controlled virtually no territory within Cambodia. Since 1982, this recognition has been transferred to the **Coalition Government of Democratic Kampuchea,** established in 1982 by the three anti-PRK factions: the Party of Democratic Kampuchea (i.e., the *Khmers Rouges*); the *Armée Nationale Sihanoukiste*; and the Khmer People's National Liberation Front.

GOVERNMENT AND PARTY LEADERSHIP

Prince Norodom Sihanouk	President
Son Sann (KPNLF)	Prime Minister
Khieu Samphan (*Khmers Rouges*)	Vice-President in charge of Foreign Affairs

Members of the co-ordination committees

National Defence: Son Sen (*Khmers Rouges*), Im Chhudeth (KPNLF), In Tam (ANS).

Military Affairs: Long Don (*Khmers Rouges*), Ea Chuor King Meng (KPNLF), Hul Sakada (ANS).

Economy and Finance: Ieng Sary (*Khmers Rouges*), Boun Sai (KPNLF), Buor Herl (ANS).

Culture and Education: Thuch Rin (*Khmers Rouges*), Chhoy Vi (KPNLF), Chak Saroeun (ANS).

Press and Information Affairs: Peth Bounreth (*Khmers Rouges*), Meak Lanh (KPNLF), Truong Mealy (ANS).

Public Health and Social Affairs: Thiounn Thioeun (*Khmers Rouges*), Bou Kheng (KPNLF), Khek Vandy (ANS).

INDEX